Camping
New Mexico

Melinda Crow

FALCON®

HELENA, MONTANA

A FALCON GUIDE ®

Falcon® Publishing is continually expanding its list of recreation guidebooks. All books include detailed descriptions, accurate maps, and all the information necessary for enjoyable trips. You can order extra copies of this book and get information and prices for other Falcon® guidebooks by writing Falcon, P.O. Box 1718, Helena, MT 59624 or calling toll free 1-800-582-2665. Also, please ask for a free copy of our current catalog. Visit our website at www.Falcon.com or contact us by e-mail at falcon@falcon.com.

All photos by the author unless otherwise noted.
Cover photo by Stewart Green.

Library of Congress Cataloging-in-Publication Data
Crow, Melinda.
    Camping New Mexico / by Melinda Crow
        p. cm.
    Includes index.
    ISBN 1-56044-709-5
        1. Camping--New Mexico--Guidebooks. 2. Camp sites, facilities, etc.--New Mexico--Guidebooks. 3. New Mexico--Guidebooks. I. Title.

GV191.42.N6 C76 1999
647.94789'09--dc21   99-22910

CAUTION

Outdoor recreational activities are by their very nature potentially hazardous. All participants in such activities must assume the responsibility for their own actions and safety. The information contained in this guidebook cannot replace sound judgment and good decision-making skills, which help reduce risk exposure, nor does the scope of this book allow for disclosure of all the potential hazards and risks involved in such activities.

Learn as much as possible about the outdoor recreational activities in which you participate, prepare for the unexpected, and be cautious. The reward will be a safer and more enjoyable experience.

♻ Text pages printed on recycled paper.

Contents

Acknowledgments

It was my pleasure during the research phase of this book to have met many wonderful people on the road. Camaraderie with fellow campers, camp hosts, and park rangers is often the highlight of my work. Without the valuable input of dedicated Forest Service personnel statewide, the content of the book would be found to be quite lacking. This was perhaps the most difficult book I have written. The reasons are many, but suffice it to say that without the undying support of my husband Gary and daughter Alyssa, completion would have been impossible. For all the fast food, for all the lonely hours while I hammered at the keyboard, and for giving me the freedom and encouragement to chase my rainbows, I thank you.

NEW MEXICO GEOGRAPHIC DIVISIONS MAP

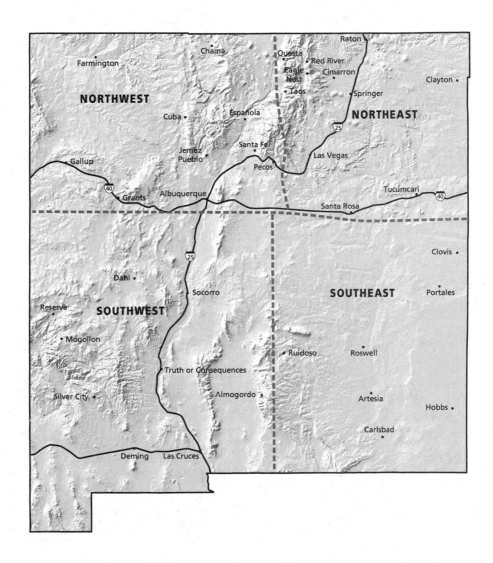

LEGEND

Interstate Highway

U.S. Highway

State or County Road

Forest Service Road

Lake

River

Intermittent River

National Park, Monument, Recreation Area

National, State Forest

Public Campgrounds

City, Town

State Border

Compass

Scale

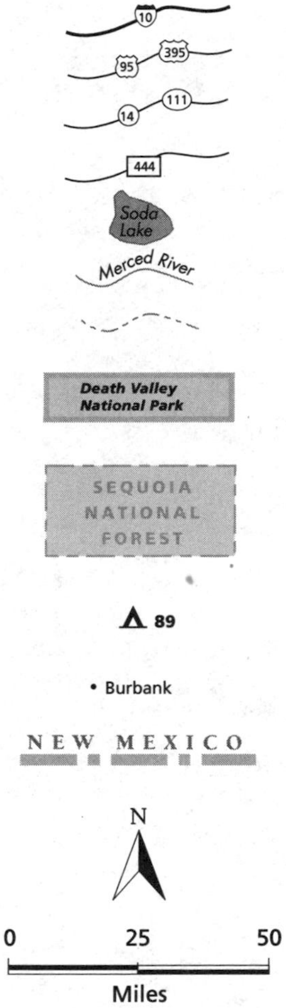
10
95
395
14
111
444
Soda Lake
Merced River
Death Valley National Park
SEQUOIA NATIONAL FOREST
89
Burbank
NEW MEXICO
N
0
25
50
Miles

About This Book

New Mexico holds the key to my heart. The rugged landscape, with its inefface-able contrast between desert and mountain, whispers sweet words to my soul. My goal in writing this book is to share with you the places that I love most.

The information in the front of the book should help familiarize you with the state, its inhabitants, and its camping choices. This book lists only public camping facilities. There are privately owned commercial campgrounds throughout the state, many of which are outstanding. But public camping remains the predominant choice of campers in New Mexico, perhaps because the opportunities are so wide-ranging. Also, only organized camping areas are described here. Backcountry camping is possible in many of the national forests and wilderness areas throughout the state. Be sure to check with rangers regarding restrictions and conditions.

For organizational purposes, I divide the state into four main regions and then into areas that contain camping choices. I give a brief description of each campground and provide contact information, should you wish to know more. The At-a-Glance tables for each area are designed to help you narrow the choices. Each campground description gives you the information you need to plan your trip. There's nothing more disheartening than arriving at a campground with fishing gear ready, only to learn that the nearest stream is five miles away. Elevations and facilities are listed as well. Rather than provide exact fees, which change frequently, the descriptions and tables provide you with a fee range, using symbols that are standard throughout the book. These ranges are based on 1999 fees and are subject to change. Many campgrounds have restrictions regarding the number of people, camping units, and vehicles per campsite. Be sure to check with the appropriate agency for specifics.

The information in this book is accurate at the time of publication, but because camping facilities change frequently, future accuracy cannot be guaranteed. If you would like to share information about changes you encounter, please send it to the author, care of Falcon Publishing, P.O. Box 1718, Helena, MT 59624. *New Mexico Magazine* has a monthly feature called, "One of Our Fifty is Missing," which contains humorous examples of how the rest of the country often forgets New Mexico. I think the real reason the state is overlooked is because New Mexico is difficult to compare to the other forty-nine states. It has an isolated beauty that places it on a plane all its own. May your travels to the Land of Enchantment be all that you wish for. The road begins here.

New Mexico Wildlife

The wildlife population in the state is as diverse as the terrain. Since camping here puts you in their habitat, it is wise to educate yourself about the local fauna.

Snakes. Diamondback rattlesnakes are perhaps the creature most feared by people traveling in the southwestern United States. The rattler can be found in all regions of New Mexico, with the greatest concentrations found at elevations below 7,000 feet. Contrary to popular belief, the rattlesnake does not love extremely hot weather. In fact its level of activity peaks around 80 to 85 degrees. For campers, this means morning or evening hikes are the time to Use the most care. If a hike takes you through grassy or brushy areas, a walking stick or broom handle is a useful defense against snakes. Prod the brush before every step. While camping in areas likely to be inhabited by snakes, make a habit of checking shoes and sleeping bags for unwanted visitors.

Bears. The only species of bear remaining in New Mexico is the black bear. These bears are either black or light cinnamon in color. Among the New Mexico bears, there are two distinct levels of sensitivity to humans. Backcountry bears range far from population centers and are quite timid in the presence of humans. They are experts at keeping out of sight unless they wish to be seen. Frontcountry bears are those that have been desensitized to humans and are in fact more likely to come into populated areas looking for a meal than to forage in the wild. Sweet treats found in coolers and garbage cans become addicting. This segment of the bear population is growing as the number of tourists increases. Frontcountry bears create a nuisance in many camping areas, but unprovoked attacks on humans are rare. Still, there are things you need to know when camping in their neighborhood.

- Follow all posted regulations concerning bears.

- Bears in New Mexico have not yet discovered that they can open car doors (as they have in other Western states), so store all food and food containers inside a closed, hard-sided vehicle. This includes canned food, beverages, pet food, coolers, and water containers.

- Store all cooking utensils in the same manner. This includes coffee pots, stoves, silverware, and dishes, no matter how clean you think they are.

- Do not bring food, cosmetics, or other toiletries into your tent or pop-up camper. Eliminate everything that has an odor.

- Do not sleep in the same clothes you cook in. Change into clean clothes and store cooking clothes in the same way you store food.

- Immediately dispose of all trash in dumpsters or bear-proof containers.

- Hiking at dusk or dawn increases your chances of encountering a bear.

- Use extra caution when hiking in places with limited visibility, such as bends in the trail.

- Make sure children and pets stay within your sight at all times.

If you encounter a bear, either in your campsite or on the trail, both you and your children need to know how to react. The old advice of playing dead applies only to the worst-case scenario in which you are actually attacked. Your goal is to avoid this by giving the bear a way out of the confrontation.

- Stay calm. Leave the area if the bear has not detected you.

- If detected, stop and slowly back away while facing the bear, without making direct eye contact. Give the bear plenty of space to escape; step off the trail if necessary. Remember that a charge is not an attack; startled bears may attempt to bluff.

- Speak softly to the bear.

- Never run! Always walk away. Running may trigger the bear's predatory instinct to give chase.

The national forest rangers are the best source of information regarding bear habits in the areas in which you plan to camp. For further reading a good choice is Falcon's *Bear Aware*, by Bill Schneider.

It's tempting to feed the friendly wildlife like these ground squirrels.

Friendly Fauna

Now that you've read all the scary stuff and may be considering vacationing elsewhere, here's the good news. New Mexico has a vast and varied population of birds and mammals that can greatly enhance your camping trip. Take a pair of binoculars, a good field guide that includes drawings of tracks, and your sense of adventure. The list of animals you might see includes deer, elk, chipmunks, squirrels, opossums, coyotes, foxes, raccoons, gophers, beavers, and rabbits. In the skies, look for hummingbirds, jays, owls, and bats, to name a few.

A word of caution is necessary here. Never leave food out for any of these creatures. The reasons are many but the best is simply to lessen our human impact on nature so that future generations can continue to enjoy its wild legacy.

New Mexico Camping Choices

Public camping choices in the state are quite varied, both in level of development and the terrain encompassed. There are campgrounds for those seeking comforts such as electricity, as well as more primitive camps with little or no development. And while there are variations, generalizations can be made about campgrounds offered by each of the governing agencies in the state. The following descriptions can help you decide where to begin your search for that perfect spot to hang your hammock:

State Parks. New Mexico's state parks are premier showcases of the state's culture, history, landscape, and recreational opportunities. If there's a large body of water involved, expect to find the New Mexico Parks Department in charge. In general, camping facilities at the state parks are a step above what you'll find at other campgrounds. Look for electrical hookups, dump stations, hot showers, and other amenities like marinas and visitor centers.

Most of the state parks operate year-round and offer hiking trails for visitors of all fitness levels. Ice fishing and wildlife watching are popular outdoor activities during the off-season. State park camping fees are slightly higher than at campgrounds maintained by other agencies. However, annual passes are available for those who spend considerable time camping at the parks in a given year.

You can expect well-designed and well-maintained facilities at all parks, and many have been recently updated.

Reservations are currently available only at Desert Cove Campground at Elephant Butte Lake State Park. However, many other campgrounds may soon be included in the reservation system due to increase in demand.

For more information:
New Mexico State Parks
Energy, Minerals, & Natural Resources Department
2040 S. Pacheco
P.O. Box 1147
Santa Fe, NM 87505
505-827-7173
888-NMP-ARKS
www.emnrd.state.nm.us/nmparks

Dispersed camping is a common choice among tent campers in many areas of the state.

U.S. Army Corps of Engineers. Two campgrounds are managed by the U.S. Army Corps of Engineers in New Mexico. As throughout the U.S., New Mexico USACE parks offer excellence in campground design and maintenance. Drinking water, showers, and some electrical hookups are among the amenities. Operations are manned by paid camp hosts who are generally knowledgeable about the facility and surrounding area.

Fees are similar to state park fees. No reservations are accepted at present, but these campgrounds may be added to the national reservation system in the future.

For more information:
U.S. Army Corps of Engineers
Albuquerque District
4101 Jefferson Plaza NE
Albuquerque, NM 87109-3435
(505) 342-3283
FAX (505) 342-3498
www.spa.usace.army.mil

National Forests. New Mexico has five national forests, encompassing almost 10 million acres. All offer campgrounds with similar facilities. Look for picnic tables, fire rings with grills, vault toilets, and, in some cases drinking water.

Many Forest Service campgrounds are scheduled for improvements to make sites more accessible and amenities more modern. Some of these changes are designed to reduce human impact on the forest. This often means fewer and smaller campgrounds with sites spaced closer together and accessible by paved roads.

While these changes will make the campgrounds more appealing to some, others may want to look into less-structured camping choices. The changes also affect dispersed camping, which is no longer allowed in some national forest areas. It is wise to check with rangers before embarking on any camping trip into a national forest.

Fees in the New Mexico national forests still remain among the lowest in the country. Many campgrounds are free, with fees at others ranging between $5 and $10 per night. The new national reservation system's inventory of New Mexico campgrounds is deficient. We can hope that the list of reservable sites expands in the future.

For more information:
Carson National Forest
208 Cruz Alta Road
Taos, NM 87571
505-758-6200

Cibola National Forest
2113 Osuna Road., NE, Suite A
Albuquerque, NM 87113-1001
505-346-2650

Gila National Forest
3005 E. Camino del Bosque
Silver City, NM 88061
505-388-8201

Lincoln National Forest
Federal Building
1101 New York
Alamogordo, NM 88310
505-434-7200

Santa Fe National Forest
1474 Rodeo Road
Santa Fe, NM 87505
505-438-7840

National Parks. There are ten national monuments, two national historical parks, and one national park in New Mexico. Organized camping operated by the National Park Service is available at only two of these parks: Bandelier National Monument and Chaco Culture National Historical Park. Additionally, backcountry camping is allowed at White Sands National Monument and at both El Morro and El Malpais national monuments.

National Park Service campgrounds are typically sparse in amenities, with the focus being on the quality of the park, rather than on the comfort of the visitor. Expect small campgrounds, tight spacing, picnic tables, and restrooms.

Having said that, keep in mind that these parks offer something you won't find anywhere else–educational opportunities ranging from archeological to geological. The campgrounds are usually designed for minimal impact on the area, so don't come here looking for luxury or extra amenities. Fees at the national parks are slightly higher than at Forest Service camps, but they remain a travel bargain. All sites operate on a first-come-first-served basis.

For more information:
National Parks Service
Intermountain Region
12795 Alameda Parkway
Denver, CO 80225
303-969-2500
www.nps.gov/parks

Bureau of Land Management. The Bureau of Land Management is the single largest landholder in the state of New Mexico. And while recreation isn't its top priority, plenty of opportunities exist. Development at Bureau of Land Management recreation sites varies widely. In general, expect only picnic tables and toilets and campgrounds that are sometimes indistinguishable from Forest Service camps.

Fees at Bureau of Land Management campgrounds mirror Forest Service fees. Many locations are free; others charge a fee that ranges between $5 and $10. No reservations are taken for these recreation areas.

For more information:
Bureau of Land Management
New Mexico State Office
1474 Rodeo Road
P.O. Box 27115
Santa Fe, NM 87502-0115
505-438-7400
www.nm.blm.gov/www/new_home_2.html

New Mexico Game and Fish Department. The camping areas managed by the Game and Fish Department are by far the most primitive in the state. Expect little more than dispersed camping on the shores of a lake, with toilet facilities provided. The good news is that these areas offer some of the best lake fishing in the state at little or no cost. Crowds are usually not a problem either.

For more information:
New Mexico Department of Game and Fish
P.O. Box 25112
Santa Fe, NM 87504
505-827-7911

Camping Etiquette

Camping rule number one is this: Remember that you are not at home, and you're usually not alone. Rule number two is this: Follow all posted rules. These rules may seem arbitrary to you, but be assured that they serve a purpose. Beyond these two, the following are a few general camping guidelines that can help make the entire camping experience more pleasant for all of us.

- **Don't offend other people's senses.** Consider the impact of everything you do on fellow campers. Every noise you make, every flashlight you shine, and every smelly pile your dog leaves behind are an interruption of someone else's pleasure.

- **Share space graciously.** The close quarters of some campgrounds force us to share everything from plumbing to parking. The best measure is to never use more than your neighbor does. Don't take up an extra parking space. Don't spread your camp to the limits. Don't hog the water or the water faucet. Nobody wants to see your dish towels or bath soap at the community water faucet.

- **Leave your campsite better than you found it.** Always do more than just clean up after yourself. Take a minute to pick up the trash left behind by the guy before you. Close all garbage cans and restroom doors.

- **Learn how to camp lightly.** This means having the least possible impact on the environment. If we are going to be allowed to continue camping in national forests and state parks, those of us who are vehicle campers would be wise to study the practices that have become standard for backcountry campers.

These rules are not designed to limit your fun, but rather to enhance everyone's long-term enjoyment of our natural resources.

Northwest

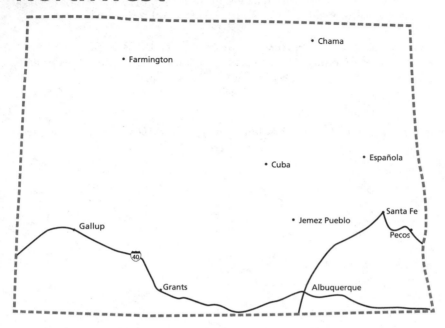

If you are looking for a place away from the crowds where you can steep your-self in the magic of a less-developed New Mexico, this is the region for you. Here you can enjoy lush, green mountains or red rock deserts, calm lakes or rushing rivers. Spend your days exploring ancient ruins or soaking away your cares in hot mineral springs. Campgrounds are numerous, but people and civilization are in somewhat short supply, so plan your trip to the northwest accordingly.

FARMINGTON

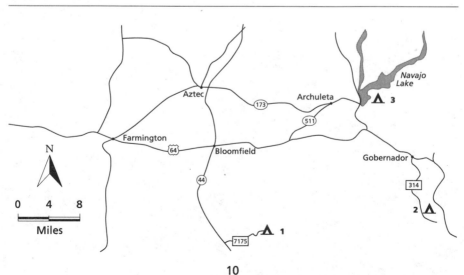

Welcome to the badlands. The northwest corner of New Mexico, the area surrounding Farmington, is harsh, rugged, and has remained mostly undisturbed for centuries. It has been home for many cultures, but never densely populated. The major landholder in the area is the Navajo Nation, followed by the Bureau of Land Management.

The city of Farmington presents a delightful venture into an authentic Southwest lifestyle that has resisted the glitz of many larger southwestern cities. Galleries, museums, and restaurants entice you to step in from the heat and slow your pace.

Heat is a critical factor in planning your camping trip to the Farmington area. High temperatures in excess of 90 degrees F throughout the summer months, combined with low humidity, create the need to consume large quantities of water, most of which must be hauled with you when camping in the area.

Camping choices near Farmington include sites on the blue waters of Navajo Lake and campgrounds at Angel Peak and Cedar Springs which allow you to fully appreciate the desert beauty.

For more information:
Farmington Convention & Visitors Bureau
2032 W. Main
Farmington, NM 87401
800-448-1240
www.farmingtonnm.org

Aztec Chamber of Commerce
203 N. Main Street
Aztec, NM 87410
Phone: 505-334-9551

FARMINGTON

	Group sites	RV sites	Total # of sites	Max. RV length	Hookups	Toilets	Showers	Drinking water	Dump station	Pets	Wheelchair	Recreation	Fee	Season	Can reserve	Stay limit
1 Angel Peak	•	•	13	16		V				•		H	$			14
2 Cedar Spring			4			V				•		HO	$	May–Nov		14
3 Navajo Lake State Park	•	•	251		WE	F	•	•	•	•	•	HSFBL	$-$$			14

Hookups: W = Water E = Electric S = Sewer
Toilets: F = Flush V = Vault P = Pit C = Chemical
Recreation: H = Hiking S = Swimming F = Fishing B = Boating L = Boat launch O = Off-highway driving R = Horseback riding
Maximum Trailer/RV Length given in feet. **Stay Limit** given in days. **Fee** $ = $0–5; $$ = $6–10; $$$ = $11–20.
If no entry under **Season**, campground is open all year. If no entry under **Fee**, camping is free.

1 Angel Peak Recreation Area

Location: 20 miles southeast of Bloomfield
Sites: 13 sites for tents and RVs
Facilities: Vault toilets, tables, grills, hiking trails
Fee per night: $
Elevation: 6,650 feet
Management: Bureau of Land Management, 505-599-8900
Activities: Hiking
Finding the campground: From the town of Bloomfield, travel south 15 miles on New Mexico 44. Turn east onto County Road 7175 and go 6 miles to the campground.

About the campground: Named for a towering rock formation, this secluded campground offers hiking trails and scenic overlooks that allow you to enjoy the sculptured rocks and rich hues of the high desert. Though understandably sparse in vegetation, the campground is adequate for a getaway. The campground and picnic areas do attract some locals, but otherwise it's quiet. This is a pack-it-in, pack-it-out camp, and no water is available.

2 Cedar Spring

Location: 56 miles southeast of Farmington
Sites: 4 sites for tents
Facilities: Vault toilets, tables, grills
Fee per night: $
Elevation: 7,300 feet
Management: Carson National Forest, Jicarilla Ranger District, 505-632-2956
Activities: Hiking, four-wheel driving
Finding the campground: From Farmington, travel east on U.S. Highway 64 about 48 miles to Gobernador. Turn south onto Forest Road 314. Go 7 miles to the campground.

About the campground: Isolation is the key here. Well off the beaten path and only large enough to accommodate three other travelers, Cedar Spring is ideal for lovers of peace and quiet. Located on the easternmost edge of the Carson National Forest, there's not much to do here but enjoy the scenery. The forest rises like an oasis against the desert backdrop to the west. Wildlife viewing opportunities should be abundant at this lonely site. No water is available.

3 Navajo Lake State Park

Location: 38 miles east of Farmington
Sites: 251 sites for tents and RVs
Facilities: The state park has a visitor center, group shelter, dump station, flush toilets, showers, marina, playground, boat launch, hiking trails, and wheelchair accessible facilities.

Fee per night: $ to $$, annual permit available
Elevation: 6,100 feet
Management: New Mexico State Parks Department, 505-632-2278; www.emnrd.state.nm.us/nmparks
Activities: Hiking, fishing, hunting, water sports, wildlife viewing, scuba diving
Finding the campground: From Farmington, travel east 34 miles on U.S. Highway 64. Turn north onto New Mexico 539. Go 4 miles to the main entrance.

About the campground: Navajo Lake is New Mexico's second largest reservoir, with more than 15,000 surface acres. Fishing is possible for a full range of cold and warm water species, including trout and kokanee salmon. There are three campgrounds, three marinas, paved trails, raised fishing platforms, and plenty of space to enjoy the outdoors.

The largest campground is Pine River. It has 160 sites, 54 with electric hookups. With the easiest access, it is by far the most popular facility at the park. The smaller, Sims Mesa campground is also a full-service area. It has 43 sites, 20 with electricity. Below the dam, you'll find the Cottonwood campground. With facilities on both sides of the San Juan River, it offers 48 campsites, 23 with electricity.
All three campgrounds have wheelchair-accessible facilities, public phones, and group shelters.

CHAMA

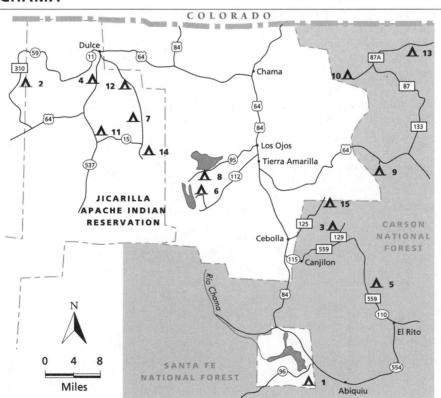

The most striking thing about the area surrounding Chama is its diversity. As you travel north through Abiquiu, the orange and red canyon walls gradually give way to pinon-dotted mesas before you reach the tall pines that grace the weathered mountains around Chama.

A list of things to do in the region includes a scenic train ride on the Cumbres & Toltec railroad, rock collecting near Abiquiu Dam, and a visit to the Tierra Wools Showroom in Los Ojos, or you can simply enjoy the natural beauty. Wildflowers are abundant in the spring, and wildlife throughout the year.

There are plenty of camping choices that allow you to fully enjoy the region. The Jicarilla Apache Indian Reservation offers camping at several lakes. Fishing here is outstanding but strictly regulated. It is advisable to obtain a complete set of these regulations before you pack for your trip.

Camping in the Carson and Santa Fe National Forests is possible at several designated campgrounds. These range in size from 4 sites to 52 and offer typical Forest Service amenities. Two state parks also provide camping and fishing opportunities: El Vado and Heron lakes are located in the Rio Chama State Recreation Area. You'll find the campgrounds at these two sites a step up from the national forest camps.

Abiquiu Lake is one of the two U.S. Army Corps of Engineers recreation facilities in New Mexico. If you've never camped at a USACE campground, consider giving it a try here at Abiquiu. The campgrounds are full-service and well-designed.

For more information:
Chama Valley Chamber of Commerce
P.O. Box 306
Chama, NM 87520
800-477-0149
www.chama.com

Jicarilla Apache Indian Reservation, Fish & Game Department
P.O. Box 313
Dulce, NM 87528
505-759-3255
www.espanola.com/g&f/fishing.htm

CHAMA

	Group sites	RV sites	Total # of sites	Max. RV length	Hookups	Toilets	Showers	Drinking water	Dump station	Pets	Wheelchair	Recreation	Fee	Season	Can reserve	Stay limit
1 Abiquiu Lake	•	•	54			F	•	•	•	•	•	HSFB	$$			14
2 Buzzard Park			4			V				•		HO	$	May–Nov		14
3 Canjilon Lakes: Upper		•	52			V	•		•	•		HF	$	May–Sept		14
4 Dulce Lake	•		12			V				•		FB	$	Apr–Nov		5
5 El Rito		•	11	22		V				•		FO	$	Apr–Nov		14
6 El Vado Lake State Park		•	54		E	F	•	•	•	•		SFBL	$$$			14
7 Enbom Lake	•		D			V				•		FB	$			
8 Heron Lake	•	•	200		WE	F	•	•	•	•	•	HSFBL	$$			14
9 Hopewell Lake State Park			6			V				•		FB	$	May–Oct		14
10 Lagunitas			12			V				•		F	$	May–Oct		14
11 LaJara Lake			D			V				•		FB	$			
12 Mundo Lake	•		D			V				•		FB	$			
13 Rio de los Pinos			4			V				•		F	$	May–Sept		14
14 Stone Lake			20			V				•		FB	$$			
15 Trout Lakes			12			V				•		F	$	May–Sept		14

Hookups: W = Water E = Electric S = Sewer
Toilets: F = Flush V = Vault P = Pit C = Chemical
Recreation: H = Hiking S = Swimming F = Fishing B = Boating L = Boat launch O = Off-highway driving R = Horseback riding
Maximum Trailer/RV Length given in feet. **Stay Limit** given in days. **Fee** $ = $0–5; $$ = $6–10; $$$ = $11–20.
If no entry under **Season**, campground is open all year. If no entry under **Fee**, camping is free.

1 Abiquiu Lake (Riana Campground)

Location: 7 miles northwest of Abiquiu
Sites: 54 sites for tents and RVs
Facilities: Flush and vault toilets, tables, grills, showers, drinking water, dump station, wheelchair-accessible sites, group sites, playground, amphitheater
Fee per night: $$
Elevation: 6,283 feet
Management: U.S. Army Corps of Engineers, 505-685-4371
Activities: Hiking, swimming, fishing, boating, rock collecting
Finding the campground: From the town of Abiquiu, travel 6 miles north on U.S. Highway 84. Turn west onto New Mexico 96. Go about one mile to the campground.

About the campground: Abiquiu Lake represents the great possibilities that can be created when humans cooperate with nature. As part of the development plan for the watershed of the Rio Grande, the dam was completed in 1963. Rather than detract from the fragile natural surroundings, the clear water now mirrors them. The contrast between red and gold carved mesas and the blue water is a work of art.

Fishing recently evolved from primarily warm-water species to cold-water species due to the larger volume of water that the reservoir now holds. Cold-water fish such as trout, walleye, and kokanee salmon are now caught regularly. A current fishing report is available online at www.spa.usace.army.mil/info/abqfish.htm.

The Riana campground offers comfort spiced with the desert scenery of the area. Spacing is acceptable and the facilities are well maintained.

2 Buzzard Park

Location: 31 miles southwest of Dulce
Sites: 4 sites for tents
Facilities: Vault toilets, tables, grills
Fee per night: $
Elevation: 7,300 feet
Management: Carson National Forest, Jicarilla Ranger Station, 505-632-2956
Activities: Hiking, four-wheel driving
Finding the campground: From Dulce, travel 18 miles southwest on U.S. Highway 64. Turn north onto Forest Road 310. Go 13 miles to the campground.

About the campground: Even the name of this campground is lonely. But if solitude is your camping objective, this is a great place to leave the crowds behind. Opportunities for hiking and off-road driving are abundant and limited only by your vehicle and your willingness to leave this lovely campground.

3 Canjilon Lakes

Location: 38 miles southeast of Chama
Sites: 52 sites for tents and RVs
Facilities: Vault toilets, drinking water, tables, fire pits, wheelchair accessible
Fee per night: $
Elevation: 9,900 feet
Management: Carson National Forest, Canjilon Ranger District, 505-684-2486
Activities: Hiking, fishing
Finding the campground: From Chama, travel south 29 miles on U.S. Highway 84. Turn east onto New Mexico 115 and go 2.5 miles to Forest Road 559. Turn north onto FR 129 and go 1 mile to the campground.

About the campground: This popular string of campgrounds is testament to man's desire to catch fish even if the road into the area isn't so great. Though not as bad now as it was in years past, the road can still get rough after spring runoff. The three campgrounds (Upper, Middle, and Lower) are scattered among the piñon and provide plenty of room to spread out. Sites are well spaced and this is one of only a few camps in the region with drinking water.

4 Dulce Lake

Location: 5 miles south of Dulce
Sites: Dispersed camping
Facilities: Vault toilets, tables, grills
Fee per night: $
Elevation: 7,046 feet
Management: Jicarilla Apache Reservation, 505-759-3255
Activities: Fishing, boating
Finding the campground: From Dulce, travel south on U.S. Highway 64 about 5 miles to the campground.

About the campground: Dulce Lake is one of a string of natural ponds and lakes that sparkle like diamonds in the desert on the Jicarilla Apache Reservation. The land here is a mix of gentle pine-covered hills and mesas, grasslands dotted with sage, and natural wetlands that are carefully preserved. Bird watching is a favorite pastime at all of the lakes on the reservation. Sightings of heron, geese, and golden eagles are common. Fishing is regulated by the reservation; it is advisable to call ahead for the specifics of these regulations before you leave home.

5 El Rito Creek

Location: 8 miles northwest of El Rito
Site: 11 sites for RVs and tents
Facilities: Vault toilets, tables, grills
Fee per night: $
Elevation: 7,300 feet
Management: Carson National Forest, El Rito Ranger Station, 505-581-4554
Activities: Fishing, four-wheel driving
Finding the campground: From the town of El Rito on New Mexico 554, travel north on NM 110 (which become Forest Road 559) for about 8 miles to the campground.

About the campground: The soul of camping in this region rests in small camps like this one that are devoid of crowds, full of pine trees, and provide a decent place to fish. When the fish aren't biting, you'll want to break out the forest service maps for a bit of exploration along the myriad of winding roads that criss-cross these mountains. If you aren't the adventurous sort, just bring along a hammock, because this is a great place to hang it.

6 Vado Lake State Park

Location: 13 miles southwest of Tierra Amarilla
Sites: 54 sites for tents and RVs
Facilities: Flush toilets, drinking water, grills, tables, visitor center, electric sites, dump station, showers, trails, marina, playground
Fee per night: $$ to $$$, annual permit available
Elevation: 6,900 feet
Management:: New Mexico State Parks Department, 505-588-7247; www.emnrd.state.nm.us/nmparks
Activities: Hiking, fishing, boating, and other water sports
Finding the campground: From Tierra Amarilla, travel west on New Mexico 572 for 1.5 miles. Turn south onto NM 112 and go 11 miles to the park road.

About the campground: Like many of New Mexico's state parks, El Vado presents you with an array of recreation choices set against a backdrop that showcases the best the state has to offer. This offers fishing, boating, water-skiing, winter cross-country skiing, and superb wildlife-watching opportunities. A five and one half-mile trail connects the park with nearby Heron Lake, and is well worth the hike.
  Facilities at the campgrounds are typical of other state parks, well-spaced, well-planned, and well-maintained.

7 Enbom Lake

Location: 11 miles southeast of Dulce
Sites: Dispersed camping
Facilities: Vault toilets, tables, grills
Fee per night: $
Elevation: 7,864 feet
Management: Jicarilla Apache Reservation, 505-759-3255
Activities: Fishing, boating
Finding the campground: From Dulce, travel south on Jicarilla Reservation Road J-8 about 11 miles to the lake.

About the campground: Another of the crown jewels of the Jicarilla Apache Reservation, Enbom languishes in the pines near the Continental Divide. Though the facilities are sparse, fishing is typically good and the scenery hard to beat.

The well-stocked lakes in the state park system make catching that first "big one" easy.

8 | Heron Lake State Park

Location: 9 miles west of Los Ojos
Sites: 200 sites for tents and RVs
Facilities: Flush toilets, electric sites, dump station, tables, grills, visitor center, group shelter, marina, trails
Fee per night: $ to $$, annual permit available
Elevation: 7,200 feet
Management: New Mexico State Parks Department, 505-588-7470; www.emnrd.state.nm.us/nmparks
Activities: Fishing, hiking, boating, and other water sports
Finding the campground: From the town of Los Ojos on U.S. Highway 84, travel west about 9 miles on New Mexico 95 to the park.

About the campground: Pack your sailboard and your wet suit when you get ready for your vacation at Heron Lake. Only no-wake speeds are allowed on the lake, and the gentle breezes entice many a sailor onto the cool waters. The setting is quiet and 100 percent New Mexico.

9 Hopewell Lake State Park

Location: 21 miles east of Tierra Amarilla
Sites: 6 sites for tents
Facilities: Vault toilets, tables, grills
Fee per night: $
Elevation: 9,600 feet
Management: Carson National Forest, Tres Piedras Ranger Station, 505-758-8678
Activities: Fishing, boating
Finding the campground: From the southern intersection of U.S. highways 64 and 84, just south of Tierra Amarilla, travel east on U.S. Highway 64 about 21 miles to the campground.

About the campground: This 14-acre, high-country lake is hard to get to but worth the trip, particularly if you want to get away from the world. The same 10,000-foot pass that makes US 64 impassible in winter makes Hopewell Lake an incredible camping spot in summer. Fishing is generally good for rainbow and brook trout. Facilities are typical of small national forest camps: sparse. But if it's solitude that you crave, you'll likely find it here among the pine trees.

10 Lagunitas

Location: 25 miles southwest of Antonito, Colorado
Sites: 12 sites for tents
Facilities: Vault toilets, tables, grills
Fee per night: $
Elevation: 10,400 feet
Management: Carson National Forest, Tres Piedras Ranger Station, 505-758-8678
Activities: Fishing
Finding the campground: From Antonito, travel south on U.S. Highway 285 about 4 miles. Turn west onto Forest Road 87, and go 21 miles to the campground.

About the campground: If you can get here, you'll love it. The road is long and dusty when it's dry and slippery when it's wet. The mountain scenery is almost unmatched anywhere in the state. Fishing for rainbow and brook trout can be outstanding in the series of lakes at the head of Lagunitas Creek, so bring a hook and a book and plan to stay awhile and enjoy the peace and quiet.

11 LaJara Lake

Location: 12 miles south of Dulce
Sites: Dispersed camping
Facilities: Vault toilets, tables, grills
Fee per night: $
Elevation: 7,305 feet
Management: Jicarilla Apache Indian Reservation, 505-759-3255
Activities: Fishing, boating
Finding the campground: From Dulce, travel southwest on U.S. Highway 64 about 9 miles. Turn south onto New Mexico Highway 537 and go 3 miles to the lake.

About the campground: Camping at this tiny lake is somewhat rough, but if fishing is your thing, a little less comfort is okay. Before you venture out, be sure to call the Fish and Game Department office at the Jicarilla Apache Indian Reservation to check current camping and fishing regulations.

12 Mundo Lake

Location: 5.5 miles south of Dulce
Sites: Dispersed camping
Facilities: Vault toilets, tables, grills
Fee per night: $
Elevation: 6,800 feet
Management: Jicarilla Apache Indian Reservation, 505-759-3255
Activities: Fishing, boating
Finding the campground: From Dulce, travel south 5.5 miles on Jicarilla Reservation Road J-8 to the lake.

About the campground: As at LaJara, camping facilities here are sparse, but the lovely setting and the opportunity to catch a trout or two can be enticing enough to bring you to this out-of-the way spot. You won't find crowds here, so bring your fishing gear and just relax.

13 Rio de los Pinos

Location: 14 miles southwest of Antonito, Colorado
Sites: 4 sites for tents
Facilities: Vault toilets, tables, grills
Fee per night: $
Elevation: 8,000 feet
Management: Carson National Forest, Tres Piedras Ranger Station, 505-758-8678
Activities: Fishing
Finding the campground: From Antonito, travel south on U.S. Highway 285 about 4 miles. Turn west onto Forest Road 87 and go 10 miles to the campground.

About the campground: Situated just outside the Los Pinos State Recreation Area, this campground has the river, it has the fish, and it has the mountains and pines. The only thing missing is you.

14 Stone Lake

Location: 17 miles southeast of Dulce
Sites: 20 sites for tents
Facilities: Vault toilets, tables, grills
Fee per night: $$
Elevation: 7,247 feet
Management: Jicarilla Apache Indian Reservation, 505-759-3255
Activities: Fishing, boating
Finding the campground: From Dulce, travel south 17 miles on Jicarilla Reservation Road J-8 to the lake.

About the campground: Stone Lake offers the most structured campground of all the Jicarilla Reservation lakes. Like the others, the setting is pleasant, the fish numerous, and the crowds relatively small.

15 Trout Lakes

Location: 8.5 miles northeast of Cebolla
Sites: 12 sites for tents
Facilities: Vault toilets, tables, grills
Fee per night: $
Elevation: 9,300 feet
Management: Carson National Forest, Canjilon Ranger Station, 505-684-2486
Activities: Fishing, nonmotorized boating
Finding the campground: From the town of Cebolla on U.S. Highway 84, travel northeast 8.5 miles on Forest Road 125 to the campground.

About the campground: The name of this string of clear mountain lakes just about says all you need to know. The trout fishing is good, the scenery even better.

CUBA

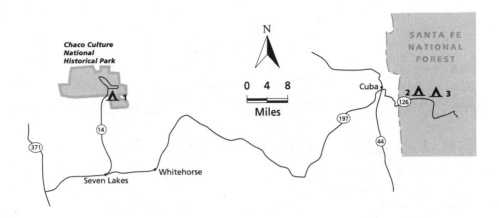

The town of Cuba is the gateway to much of New Mexico's Indian culture to the west and the lush national forests to the east. The town itself is small but serves as the commercial center for the eastern edge of the Navajo Nation.

The name "Cuba" means large tank or vat. According to Indian legend, the area was once completely filled with water. Land formations to the west bear out that story in fossil-bearing layers of red silt and clay.

All roads east lead into the Santa Fe National Forest and to the edge of the San Pedro Parks Wilderness Area, where the fishing is world-class and the scenery idyllic.

For more information:
Cuba Chamber of Commerce
P.O. Box 1000
Cuba, NM 87013
505-289-3514

Cuba Visitors Center
P.O. Box 56
Cuba, NM 87013
505-289-3808

CUBA

	Group sites	RV sites	Total # of sites	Max. RV length	Hookups	Toilets	Showers	Drinking water	Dump station	Pets	Wheelchair	Recreation	Fee	Season	Can reserve	Stay limit
1 Chaco Culture NHP	•	•	68	30		F		•	•	•	•	H	$$			7
2 Clear Creek		•	12	30		V		•		•	•	HF	$	May–Oct		14
3 Rio de las Vacas		•	15	16		V		•		•		HF	$	May–Oct		14

1 Chaco Culture National Historical Park

Location: 87 miles west of Cuba
Sites: 68 sites for tents and RVs
Facilities: Flush toilets, dump station, visitor center, group sites, wheelchair-accessible sites
Fee per night: $$
Elevation: 6,300 feet
Management: National Park Service, 505-786-7014, www.nps.gov/chcu/
Activities: Hiking, exploring historical ruins, biking
Finding the campground: From Cuba, travel west on New Mexico 197 (which becomes N-9), about 67 miles to Seven Lakes. Turn north onto N-14, following the signs 20 miles to the park.

About the campground: This premier archeological park is breathtaking in its historical beauty. The multistory dwellings found here present an unrivaled example of Pueblo pre-Columbian civilization. Come here looking for the history, not for the facilities. The last twenty miles of road are dirt; let that be a signal to the level of amenities at the park. Sites have tables and fire rings, but not much else. Drinking water is available only at the visitor center, so it's best to bring your own. You must also bring your own firewood or charcoal; none is available at the campground.

In addition to the eight self-guided trails through the ruins, hikers will find four backcountry trails to more remote areas of the canyon. There are also designated bicycle trails. As a word of caution, this is harsh terrain, with an even harsher climate. To more fully enjoy your visit to Chaco, plan and pack wisely.

2 Clear Creek

Location: 12 miles east of Cuba
Sites: 12 sites for tents and RVs
Facilities: Vault toilets, drinking water, tables, grills
Fee per night: $
Elevation: 8,500 feet
Management: Santa Fe National Forest, Cuba Ranger District, 505-289-3264
Activities: Hiking, fishing
Finding the campground: From Cuba, travel east on New Mexico Highway 126 (which becomes Forest Road 126) about 12 miles to the campground.

About the campground: The western edge of the Santa Fe National Forest is "the road less traveled" that you've been longing for. The once busy mining and logging roads are now rutted and all but abandoned. Of course, that means heaven to four-wheel drive enthusiasts. Using Forest Service maps, you could explore for days and not run out of roads. Rockhounds will thrill at narrow tracks littered with malachite slivers. Wildlife watchers can set their scopes on black bear and deer that have had little exposure to humans. The campground is small, but pine-shaded sites offer a bit of space between campers.

3 Rio de las Vacas

Location: 13 miles east of Cuba
Sites: 15 sites for tents and RVs
Facilities: Vault toilets, drinking water, tables, grills
Fee per night: $
Elevation: 8,500 feet
Management: Santa Fe National Forest, Cuba Ranger District, 505-289-3264
Activities: Hiking, fishing
Finding the campground: From Cuba, travel east on New Mexico Highway 126 (which becomes Forest Road 126) about 13 miles to the campground.

About the campground: Like its neighbor (Clear Creek), Rio de las Vacas offers the outdoor adventurer a retreat from the crowded eastern half of the state and a look at New Mexico's national forests as they were several decades ago. The added bonus here is access to Rio de las Vacas, which offers decent trout fishing.

JEMEZ SPRINGS

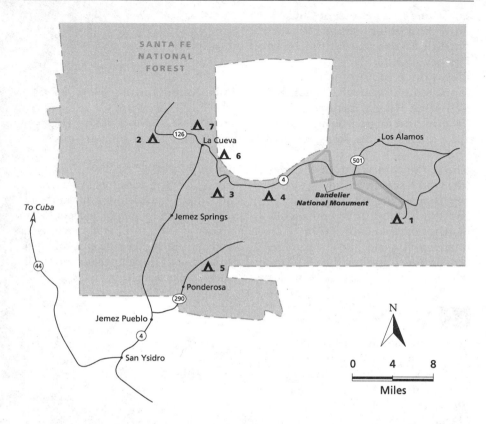

If you don't know the Jemez Springs area, it's no surprise, because not a lot of people do. Finding it is like discovering the place where the locals hang out just around the bend from the high profile places to which the tourists flock. As you enter Jemez country, you pass through the Jemez Pueblo Reservation. The red canyon walls set the stage for your journey into the magical valley. You can't really experience Jemez until you've had Indian fry bread dripping with honey, so go ahead and stop at the roadside stands.

The bread is just the beginning of what could lead to sensory overload if your visit to Jemez is too rushed. Slow down and enjoy the sights and the people. Stop at Soda Dam, a naturally formed mineral dam that resembles cave formations usually found deep in the earth. Hike to Jemez Falls (there's a long trail and a short one). Visit the hot springs (if you're the adventurous sort) or one of the state's premier wineries in Ponderosa. Tour the Seven Springs Fish Hatchery. Eat a green chile burger in La Cueva. Take a relaxing mineral bath and massage at the local bathhouse. Want more to do? How about a scenic drive to the Gilman Tunnels? Or perhaps an afternoon collecting Apache tears (small pebbles of obsidian)? There's always an educational visit to Bandelier National Monument. Still not enough? You could always cast a line in the Jemez River and while away the hours hauling in the trout.

For more information:
Jemez Springs Bath House
062 Jemez Springs Plaza
P.O. Box 112
Jemez Springs, NM 87025
www.jemez.com/baths/

JEMEZ SPRINGS

		Group sites	RV sites	Total # of sites	Max. RV length	Hookups	Toilets	Showers	Drinking water	Dump station	Pets	Wheelchair	Recreation	Fee	Season	Can reserve	Stay limit
1	Bandelier NM	•	•	94			F	•	•	•	•	•	HFR	$$	Apr–Oct		7
2	Fenton Lake SP	•	•	40		WE	V		•		•	•	HFB	$-$$			14
3	Jemez Falls		•	52	22		V		•		•	•	HF	$$		•	14
4	Las Conchas			12			V		•		•		HF	$$			14
5	Paliza	•	•	3	16		V		•		•		HO	$$		•	14
6	Redondo		•	60	45		V		•		•		H	$$		•	14
7	San Antonio		•	47	35		V		•		•		H	$$		•	14

Hookups: W = Water E = Electric S = Sewer
Toilets: F = Flush V = Vault P = Pit C = Chemical
Recreation: H = Hiking S = Swimming F = Fishing B = Boating L = Boat launch O = Off-highway driving R = Horseback riding
Maximum Trailer/RV Length given in feet. **Stay Limit** given in days. **Fee** $ = $0–5; $$ = $6–10; $$$ = $11–20.
If no entry under **Season,** campground is open all year. If no entry under **Fee,** camping is free.

1 Bandelier National Monument

Location: 10 miles southeast of Los Alamos
Sites: 94 sites for tents and RVs
Facilities: Flush toilets, drinking water, tables, grills, group sites, dump station
Fee per night: $$
Elevation: 6,700 feet
Management: National Park Service, 505-672-0343, www.nps.gov/band/
Activities: Hiking, fishing, horseback riding, exploring historical sites
Finding the campground: From Los Alamos, travel about 5 miles south on New Mexico Highway 501. Turn east onto NM 4 and go about 5 miles to the park entrance.

About the campground: The opportunity to visit thirteenth-century Pueblo Indian cliff dwellings doesn't come along every day. If you're in the Jemez area, it's worth the drive to this monument.

The campground itself is nothing out of the ordinary. Typical of the National Park Service, emphasis is on experiencing the location with as little disruption of natural surroundings as possible. For the adventurous, however, there are over 70 miles of hiking trails that provide additional camping opportunities in the backcountry of the monument. If you are willing to forego the comforts of vehicle camping, this is the best way to truly enjoy the sights that Bandelier has to offer.

2 Fenton Lake State Park

Location: 13 miles northwest of Jemez Springs
Sites: 40 sites for tents and RVs
Facilities: Vault toilets, drinking water, tables, grills, group sites, wheelchair-accessible sites, electricity, playground
Fee per night: $ to $$, annual permit available
Elevation: 7,900 feet
Management: New Mexico State Parks Department, 505-829-3630, www.emnrd.state.nm.us/nmparks
Activities: Hiking, fishing, boating, snowmobiling, cross-country skiing and ice fishing in winter
Finding the campground: From Jemez Springs, travel north on New Mexico Highway 4 about 8 miles to the village of La Cueva. Turn west onto NM 126 (which becomes Forest Road 126) and go about 5 miles to the park entrance.

About the campground: If you have plans to see the sights and enjoy the activities in the Jemez area, it will be difficult to do from here. The problem isn't access, but rather lack of willingness to leave once you get here. The lake and surrounding scenery create an idyllic location for doing a whole lot of nothing. The fishing is good, especially if you bring a canoe. If the fish aren't biting, the combination of Ponderosa pines and prolific wildflowers provides the perfect place to nap.

The campground is laid out much like a national forest camp, with the bonus of some sites with electric hookups. With 40 sites to choose from, almost all with views of the lake, there's bound to be one to your liking.

3 Jemez Falls

Location: 15 miles northeast of Jemez Springs
Sites: 52 sites for tents and RVs
Facilities: Vault toilets, drinking water, tables, grills, group sites, wheel-chair-accessible sites
Fee per night: $$
Elevation: 7,900 feet
Management: Santa Fe National Forest, Jemez Ranger District, 505-829-3535
Reservations: 1-877-444-6777, www.reserveusa.com
Activities: Hiking, fishing
Finding the campground: From Jemez Springs, travel 15 miles north and then east on New Mexico Highway 4 to the campground entrance.

About the campground: The sites at this camp are well spaced among the pines, with the added attraction of a short trail leading to the falls. Trail 137 is a wonderful hike (1.5 miles) that takes you back across the mountain to the east, ending at Battleship Rock. Overall, the camp is a near-perfect spot from which to enjoy everything the Jemez Valley has to offer. Reservations are necessary if your visit includes a weekend.

4 Las Conchas

Location: 15.5 miles northeast of Jemez Springs
Sites: 12 sites for tents
Facilities: Vault toilets, drinking water, tables, grills
Fee per night: $$
Elevation: 8,400 feet
Management: Santa Fe National Forest, Jemez Ranger District, 505-829-3535
Activities: Hiking, fishing
Finding the campground: From Jemez Springs, travel north, then east 15.5 miles on New Mexico Highway 4 to the campground.

About the campground: Las Conchas is a midsized camp compared to many of the sprawling camps closer to the action in the valley. It could be the best choice if you want a bit more solitude. You can hear the pines whispering and the mountain bluebirds calling.

5 Paliza

Location: 7.5 miles northeast of Jemez Pueblo
Sites: 3 sites for tents and small trailers, plus dispersed camping and group site
Facilities: Vault toilets, drinking water, tables, grills, group sites
Fee per night: $$
Elevation: 5,800 feet
Management: Santa Fe National Forest, Jemez Ranger District, 505-829-3535
Reservations: 1-877-444-6777, www.reserveusa.com
Activities: Hiking, four-wheel driving, rock collecting, wildlife viewing
Finding the campground: At Jemez Pueblo (not Jemez Springs), turn east onto New Mexico Highway 290 (which becomes Forest Road 266) and go 7.5 miles to the campground.

About the campground: Don't care about fishing? Just looking for a place to escape the crowds? Paliza is calling your name. This is the only camp in the western Santa Fe National Forest that offers three-sided Adirondack shelters with stone fireplaces. There are only three available, so reservations are highly recommended. There is room for small and medium-sized trailers to park next to the shelters. There are also tent sites scattered across the hillside.

Bring your binoculars because the wildlife at this isolated camp is abundant. Daytime hours treat you to huge numbers of hummingbirds, while dusk signals the graceful airborne dance of bats that live in nearby cliffside caves.

Adirondack shelters like this one at Paliza are a treat at some campgrounds in the Santa Fe National Forest.

6 Redondo

Location: 11 miles northeast of Jemez Springs
Sites: 60 sites for tents and RVs.
Facilities: Vault toilets, drinking water, tables, grills
Fee per night: $$
Elevation: 8,100 feet
Management: Santa Fe National Forest, Jemez Ranger District, 505-829-3535
Reservations: 1-877-444-6777, www.reserveusa.com
Activities: Hiking, scenic driving
Finding the campground: From Jemez Springs, travel 11 miles north, then east on New Mexico Highway 4 to the campground.

About the campground: Like the campground at Jemez falls, Redondo puts you in the middle of the action. Anything you'd want to do in the valley is a short drive away. The camp is large, but the sites are well spaced to provide some privacy.

7 | San Antonio

Location: 9.5 miles north of Jemez Springs
Sites: 47 sites for tents and RVs
Facilities: Vault toilets, drinking water, tables, grills
Fee per night: $$
Elevation: 6,800 feet
Management: Santa Fe National Forest, Jemez Ranger District, 505-829-3535
Reservations: 1-877-444-6777, www.reserveusa.com
Activities: Hiking, fishing
Finding the campground: From Jemez Springs, travel 7.5 miles north on New Mexico Highway 4 to the village of La Cueva. Turn west onto NM 126 and go 2 miles to the campground.

About the campground: Break out the hammock for this campground. It perches on the hillside among the pines and aspens and has a relaxing feel. It's still close enough to the action in the valley that you can fish, hike, or be a tourist easily (after your nap, that is.)

ESPAÑOLA–SANTA FE

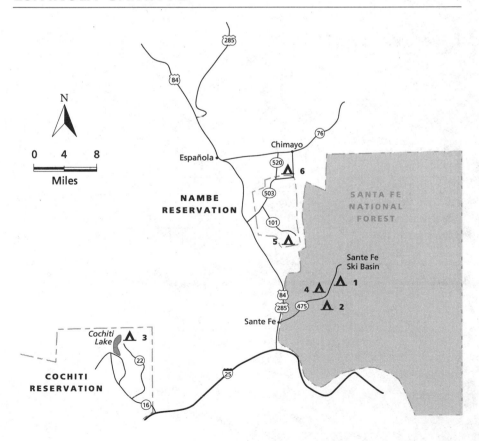

If you're considering a camping vacation to this area, you've chosen the heart of New Mexico. It's all here: aspens and pines, mountains, food, art, and air so fresh you can almost taste it. The downside to traveling in and around Santa Fe is that you are not alone in your quest for a New Mexican adventure. Visitors flock here by the thousands, swelling the city to twice its normal size on summer weekends. Camping in the surrounding mountains is one way to lose part of the crowd, but rest assured, not all.

The best way to get away from fellow travelers is to venture onto forest roads and hiking trails, both of which are abundant in the area. Then after a long day's trek you can fully appreciate the joy of companionship and the flavors of Santa Fe.

For more information:
Santa Fe County Chamber of Commerce
510 N. Guadalupe Street, Suite N
Santa Fe, NM 87501
505-983-7317
www.santafechamber.com

Española Valley Chamber of Commerce
417 Big Rock Center
Española, NM 87532
505-753-2831

ESPAÑOLA–SANTA FE

		Group sites	RV sites	Total # of sites	Max. RV length	Hookups	Toilets	Showers	Drinking water	Dump station	Pets	Wheelchair	Recreation	Fee	Season	Can reserve	Stay limit
1	Big Tesuque		•	7			V			•	•	HF	$$	May–Oct		14
2	Black Canyon		•	24			V	•		•	•	H	$$	May–Oct	•	14
3	Cochiti Lake		•	141		WE	F	•	•	•	•	HSFBL	$$			14
4	Hyde Memorial SP		•	44		E	V	•	•	•	•	H	$-$$			14
5	Nambe Falls			D	22	E	V	•				HF	$$$	Mar–Oct		14
6	Santa Cruz Lake			D			V	•		•	•	HSF	$$			14

Hookups: W = Water E = Electric S = Sewer
Toilets: F = Flush V = Vault P = Pit C = Chemical
Recreation: H = Hiking S = Swimming F = Fishing B = Boating L = Boat launch O = Off-highway driving R = Horseback riding
Maximum Trailer/RV Length given in feet. **Stay Limit** given in days. **Fee** $ = $0–5; $$ = $6–10; $$$ = $11–20.
If no entry under **Season,** campground is open all year. If no entry under **Fee,** camping is free.

1 Big Tesuque

Location: 11 miles northeast of Santa Fe
Sites: 7 sites for tents and RVs
Facilities: Vault toilets, grills, tables
Fee per night: $$
Elevation: 9,700 feet
Management: Santa Fe National Forest, 505-438-7801
Activities: Hiking, fishing
Finding the campground: In Santa Fe, from I-25 exit 282, travel north on U.S. Highway 285/84 for 3.6 miles to New Mexico Highway 475 (Hyde Park Road). Turn east, following the signs to the Santa Fe Ski Basin and go about 11 miles to the campground.

About the campground: Big Tesuque (tess-su-kee) is one of a string of campgrounds on Hyde Park Road on the way to the Santa Fe Ski Basin. The pines and aspen reign over a land of winding streams, gentle waterfalls, and busy wildlife. Spend a day here and you begin to understand why artists flock to the area: the place itself is an inspiring work of art.

2 Black Canyon

Location: 7.5 miles northeast of Santa Fe
Sites: 24 sites for tents and RVs
Facilities: Vault toilets, grills, tables, drinking water
Fee per night: $$
Elevation: 8,400 feet
Management: Santa Fe National Forest, 505-753-7331
Reservations: 877-444-6777, www.reserveusa.com, $8.65 fee
Activities: Hiking
Finding the campground: In Santa Fe, from I-25 exit 282, travel north 3.6 miles on U.S. Highway 285/84 to New Mexico Highway 475 (Hyde Park Road). Turn east, following the signs to the Santa Fe Ski Basin, and go about 7.5 miles to the campground.

About the campground: Reservations at Black Canyon are strongly encouraged. During the busy summer months, it is virtually the only way to secure a spot at this lovely but crowded camp. It's a nice place to lay your head after a day wandering the Santa Fe National Forest or perhaps the Pecos Wilderness, which is easily accessible via trails nearby.

3 Cochiti Lake

Location: 30 miles west of Santa Fe
Sites: 141 sites for tents and RVs
Facilities: Flush & vault toilets, tables, fire rings, boat launch, showers, dump station, drinking water
Fee per night: $$
Elevation: 5,232 feet
Management: United States Army Corps of Engineers, 505-465-0307, www.spa.usace.army.mil/cochiti/
Activities: Hiking, swimming, fishing, boating, golf
Finding the campground: Follow I-25 south of Santa Fe, and take exit 264. Turn north onto New Mexico Highway 16, then west onto New Mexico Highway 22 and follow the signs 11 miles north to the lake.

About the campground: The ashen mesas surrounding Cochiti balance the blue waters of this flood control lake, which was built in 1975. The water beckons New Mexicans seeking relief from the summer heat, so don't come here to get away from the crowds; come instead to join the fun.

   The campground facilities are certainly adequate for those looking for desert mountain scenery and water activities. Most of the roads are paved, many of the campsites have shelters, and some even have electrical hookups. Typical of Corps of Engineers campgrounds, the design and layout provide spacious sites to handle the crowds. The nearby Cochiti Lake Golf Course is public and provides a pleasant way of passing the time if the fish aren't biting.

4 Hyde Memorial State Park

Location: 8.5 miles northeast of Santa Fe
Sites: 44 sites for tents and RVs
Facilities: Vault toilets, tables, grills, sites with electricity, visitor center, playground, dump station
Fee per night: $ to $$, annual permit available
Elevation: 8,500 feet
Management: New Mexico State Parks Department, 505-983-7175, www.emnrd.state.nm.us/nmparks
Activities: Hiking, cross-country skiing, snowmobiling
Finding the campground: From I-25 in Santa Fe, take exit 282, and travel north 3.6 miles on U.S. Highway 285/84 to New Mexico Highway 475 (Hyde Park Road). Turn east, following the signs to the Santa Fe Ski Basin, and go about 8.5 miles to the campground.

About the campground: The Sangre de Cristo Mountains beg you to stop and stay awhile. The perfect balance of pine and aspen contrasts sharply with gray rock walls. The nice part is that it's hard to see and do it all. There's always a trail to save for next time, always another adventure waiting. Hyde Park makes a great place from which to begin your explorations. The sites are well spaced and some have electrical hookups; others have three-sided Adirondack shelters for that extra bit of comfort you crave.

5 | Nambe Falls

Location: 16 miles southeast of Española
Sites: Dispersed
Facilities: Vault toilets, drinking water, tables, grills, electricity
Fee per night: $$$
Elevation: 6,600 feet
Management: Nambe Pueblo, 505-455-2036
Activities: Hiking, fishing
Finding the campground: From Española, travel southeast 8.5 miles on U.S. Highway 285/84. Turn east onto New Mexico Highway 503 and go 2.5 miles to Reservation Road 101. Turn south and go 5.5 miles to the campground.

About the campground: The campground at this scenic lake is small but continually improving. Because it is a bit out of the way, it doesn't attract as many of the Santa Fe tourists as you'll find in other campgrounds in the region. Come here to relax and enjoy the quiet of the mountains.

6 | Santa Cruz Lake

Location: 13 miles east of Española
Sites: Dispersed
Facilities: Vault toilets, grills, picnic tables, drinking water
Fee per night: $$
Elevation: 6,400 feet
Management: Bureau of Land Management, 505-758-8851
Activities: Hiking, swimming, fishing
Finding the campground: From Española, travel 10 miles east on New Mexico Highway 76. Turn south onto NM 503 and go 1 mile to the campground access road.

About the campground: With the Sangre de Cristo Mountains as a backdrop, Santa Cruz Lake provides a quiet, low-altitude retreat for fishing or perhaps sailboarding. The lake is designated as a no-wake area.

Gallup

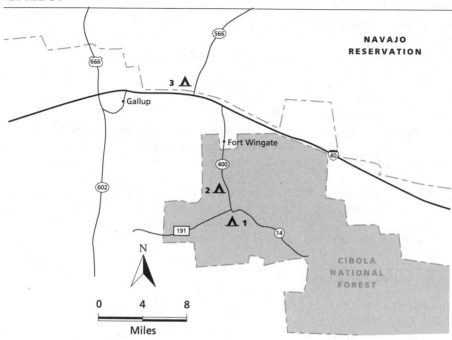

The far western reaches of New Mexico present an interesting blend of dusty red rock formations and pine forests, Native American history, and modern technology. Come here looking for blue sky and you'll find it in abundance over stretches of undeveloped land.

For more information:

Gallup Convention and Visitors Bureau:

P.O. Box 600

Gallup, NM 87305

505-863-3841

800-242-4282

www.gallupnm.org

GALLUP

	Group sites	RV sites	Total # of sites	Max. RV length	Hookups	Toilets	Showers	Drinking water	Dump station	Pets	Wheelchair	Recreation	Fee	Season	Can reserve	Stay limit
1 McGaffey	•	•	49		E	V		•	•	•	•	HF	$$		•	14
2 Quaking Aspen		•	20	22		V		•		•		H	$$	May–Oct		14
3 Red Rock State Park		•	106		EW	F	•	•	•	•	•		$-$$			14

Hookups: W = Water E = Electric S = Sewer
Toilets: F = Flush V = Vault P = Pit C = Chemical
Recreation: H = Hiking S = Swimming F = Fishing B = Boating L = Boat launch O = Off-highway driving R = Horseback riding
Maximum Trailer/RV Length given in feet. **Stay Limit** given in days. **Fee** $ = $0–5; $$ = $6–10; $$$ = $11–20.
If no entry under **Season**, campground is open all year. If no entry under **Fee**, camping is free.

1 McGaffey

Paved access

Location: 22 miles southeast of Gallup
Sites: 49 sites for tents and RVs
Facilities: Vault toilets, tables, grills, drinking water, electricity, dump station
Fee per night: $$
Elevation: 8,000 feet
Management: Cibola National Forest, Mt. Taylor Ranger District, 505-287-8833
Reservations: For group facilities only, 877-444-6777, www.reserveusa.com, fee.
Activities: Hiking, fishing
Finding the campground: From I-40, take exit 33 (11 miles east of Gallup); and travel south on New Mexico Highway 400 for about 11 miles to the campground.

About the campground: This is a very popular spot. The pines and scrub oaks offer a peaceful setting, the hiking is suitable for all skill levels, and the fishing is usually adequate for most anglers. McGaffey Lake is designated as no-wake.

McGaffey is one of the few national forest camps in the state with conveniences like electric hookups and an RV dump station, and like most campgrounds in popular areas, McGaffey fills to capacity during the height of the season.

2 Quaking Aspen

Paved Road

Location: 20 miles southeast of Gallup
Sites: 20 sites for tents and RVs
Facilities: Vault toilets, tables, grills, drinking water
Fee per night: $$
Elevation: 7,600 feet
Management: Cibola National Forest, Mt. Taylor Ranger District, 505-287-8833
Activities: Hiking

Finding the campground: From Gallup, take I-40 east 11 miles to exit 33; then travel south on New Mexico Highway 400 for about 9 miles to the campground.

About the campground: Like its neighbor McGaffey, Quaking Aspen is popular due in part to the easy access to I-40. The scenery and fishing are additional drawing cards here. Either of these two camps makes a nice place to meet friends for a long weekend, but plan to arrive early to secure campsites.

3 Red Rock State Park

Location: 9 miles east of Gallup
Sites: 106 sites for tents and RVs
Facilities: Flush toilets, tables, grills, drinking water, electricity
Fee per night: $ to $$
Elevation: 6,600 feet
Management: City of Gallup, 505-722-3829, www.ci.gallup.nm.us/rrsp/00182_redrock.html
Activities: Scenic driving, rodeos, festivals
Finding the Campground: From Gallup, take I-40 east to exit 31 at Navajo Wingate Village. The park entrance is on the service road near the exit ramp.

About the campground: Located on the grounds of the annual Inter-tribal Ceremonial gathering, this state park is operated by the city of Gallup and makes an ideal stopover for travelers crossing the state on I-40. The facilities are adequate and the surrounding, sculptured red rock formations and cliffs provide a postcard setting.

GRANTS

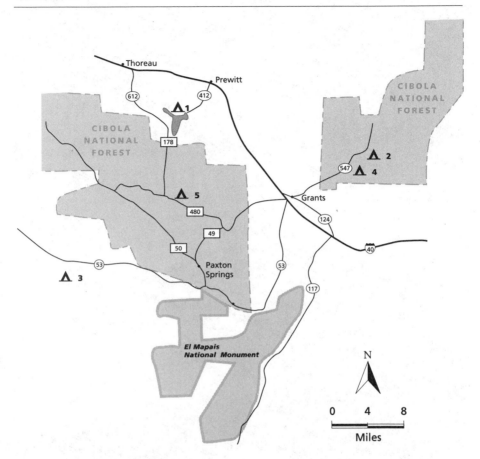

Grants is the oasis in the desert of western New Mexico and has a mixed history of logging, mining, railroading, and pure Wild West. Positioned in the shadow of 11,000-foot Mount Taylor, the city is a perfect place from which to venture off Interstate 40 to the north or south. The campgrounds here aren't always crowded, the scenery and activities match those found anywhere in the state, and the fish are just begging to be caught.

After you've caught your limit, area attractions include the Bandera Crater and Ice Caves, El Malpais National Monument, Acoma "Sky City" Pueblo, and the New Mexico Museum of Mining.

For more information:
Grants/Cibola County Chamber of Commerce
800-748-2142
www.grants.org

This mist-shrouded hilltop near Mount Taylor is typical of the scenery found in the mountainous regions of far-western New Mexico.

GRANTS

	Group sites	RV sites	Total # of sites	Max. RV length	Hookups	Toilets	Showers	Drinking water	Dump station	Pets	Wheelchair	Recreation	Fee	Season	Can reserve	Stay limit
1 Bluewater Lake State Park	•	•	120		E	F	•	•	•	•	•	HFBL	$$$			14
2 Coal Mine		•	17	22		V		•		•		H	$$	May–Sept	•	14
3 El Morro NM			9			F		•		•		H	$$			14
4 Lobo Canyon	•		9			V						H	$	May–Sept		14
5 Ojo Redondo		•	14	20		V				•		RO	$$			14

Hookups: W = Water E = Electric S = Sewer
Toilets: F = Flush V = Vault P = Pit C = Chemical
Recreation: H = Hiking S = Swimming F = Fishing B = Boating L = Boat launch O = Off-highway driving R = Horseback riding
Maximum Trailer/RV Length given in feet. **Stay Limit** given in days. **Fee** $ = $0–5; $$ = $6–10; $$$ = $11–20.
If no entry under **Season,** campground is open all year. If no entry under **Fee,** camping is free.

1 Bluewater Lake State Park

Location: 28 miles northwest of Grants
Sites: 120 sites for tents and RVs
Facilities: Flush toilets, tables, grills, group sites, dump station, showers, drinking water, boat launch
Fee per night: $ to $$, annual permit available
Elevation: 7,400 feet
Management: New Mexico State Parks Department, 505-876-2391, www.emnrd.state.nm.us/nmparks
Activities: Hiking, fishing, boating, horseback riding
Finding the campground: From I-40 west of Grants, take exit 63. Travel south on New Mexico Highway 412 about 6 miles to the park.

About the campground: Bluewater is aptly named. The cool waters attract visitors seeking relief from the summer heat, making this a very popular campground. The 120 campsites are often filled to capacity, but early arrival can assure you a choice spot. Water sports are a popular pastime at Bluewater, so bring your skis and windsurfer.

The campsites, which are scattered near the shore among piñons and juniper trees, have sheltered picnic tables and plenty of space.

2 Coal Mine

Location: 10 miles northeast of Grants
Sites: 17 sites for tents and RVs
Facilities: Vault toilets, tables, grills, drinking water
Fee per night: $$
Elevation: 7,400 feet
Management: Cibola National Forest, Mt. Taylor Ranger District, 505-287-8833
Reservations: 877-444-6777, www.reserveusa.com, fee
Activities: Hiking, scenic driving
Finding the campground: From Grants, go north on Lobo Canyon Road (New Mexico Highway 547) about 10 miles to the campground.

About the campground: Want to camp on the side of Mount Taylor? Here's your chance. Coal Mine offers all the comforts of developed camping in the Cibola National Forest, and primitive camping is possible throughout this region of the Cibola as well. Either choice is fine if all you want to do is get away from the crowds.

3 El Morro National Monument

Location: 50 miles southwest of Grants
Sites: 9 sites for tents only
Facilities: Flush toilets, tables, grills, drinking water, visitor center, museum, hiking trails
Fee per night: $$
Elevation: 7,200 feet
Management: National Parks Service, 505-783-4226, www.nps.gov/elmo/index.htm
Activities: Hiking
Finding the campground: From Grants, travel south then west about 50 miles on New Mexico Highway 53 to the campground.

About the campground: El Morro is a shrine to graffiti: A single sandstone mesa rises like a pinnacle from the desert floor emblazoned with the signs of travelers spanning the centuries. From prehistoric man to the U.S. Army Camel Corps, they all left their mark.

Like many national monuments, camping comforts are minimal. The emphasis is on enjoying the history and setting. If you enjoy either, this is the place for you.

4 Lobo Canyon

Location: 9 miles northeast of Grants
Sites: 9 sites for tents
Facilities: Vault toilets, tables, grills
Fee per night: $
Elevation: 7,400 feet
Management: Cibola National Forest, Mt. Taylor Ranger District, 505-287-8833
Activities: Hiking, scenic driving
Finding the campground: From Grants, go north on Lobo Canyon Road (New Mexico Highway 547) about 10 miles to Forest Road 239. Turn south and go 1 mile to the campground.

About the campground: These nine sites are just one more chance to spend the night in this rather secluded area of the Cibola National Forest. The crowds aren't usually a problem, except perhaps locals on picnics. Spend the day watching the wildlife or traveling the numerous forest roads that crisscross the area. (They are slippery when wet!)

Lobo Canyon also makes a convenient place to camp and make day trips to the major attractions of the area.

5 Ojo Redondo

Location: 17 miles southwest of Grants
Sites: 14 sites for tents and RVs
Facilities: Vault toilets, tables, grills
Fee per night: $$
Elevation: 8,900 feet
Management: Cibola National Forest, Mt. Taylor Ranger District, 505-287-8833
Activities: Hiking, scenic driving
Finding the campground: From Grants, travel south 10 miles on Forest Road 49 (Zuni Canyon Road). Turn west onto FR 480 and go 7 miles to the campground.

About the campground: If you like to get far away from the crowds, then this campground is for you. Getting here won't be easy, but it is a gorgeous drive that winds through piñon-covered canyons dotted by stray lava flows. Enjoy the ride.

ALBUQUERQUE

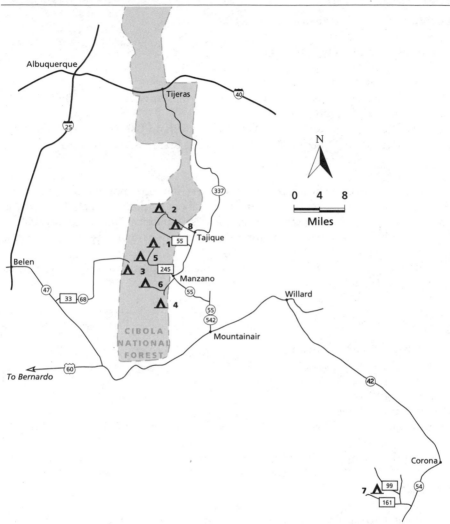

To say that Albuquerque has it all is an understatement. It is the population center of the state and has the usual attractions of a big city with the added bonus of being located in the shadow of 10,000-foot Sandia Peak. It is unfortunate that there are no camping facilities in the Sandia Mountains, but day trips are easily accomplished from the existing campgrounds farther south. A trip to Sandia Crest, whether by car or tram, is a must for visitors to the Albuquerque area. It affords nonhikers the unequaled thrill of standing on a windswept mountaintop.

Public camping in the area is all southeast of the city in the Manzano Mountains. These mountains may lack the grandeur of the Sandias, but they still present hikers, campers, and even equestrians with the opportunity to explore this region of the Cibola National Forest.

For more information:
Albuquerque Convention and Visitor's Bureau
P.O. Box 26866
Albuquerque, NM 87125-6866
800-284-2282
www.abqcvb.org

ALBUQUERQUE

		Group sites	RV sites	Total # of sites	Max. RV length	Hookups	Toilets	Showers	Drinking water	Dump station	Pets	Wheelchair	Recreation	Fee	Season	Can reserve	Stay limit
1	Capilla Peak		•	8	16		V				•		HR	$	May–Sept		14
2	Fourth of July		•	26			V	•		•	•	•	H	$$	Apr–Nov		14
3	John F. Kennedy		•	18	22		V	•			•		HR	$			14
4	Manzano Mountains SP	•	•	17		E	F	•	•	•	•	•	HR	$-$$			14
5	New Canyon		•	10	22		V	•			•		H	$	Apr–Nov		14
6	Red Canyon		•	50			V	•		•	•	•	HR	$	Apr–Nov		14
7	Red Cloud			4	22		V				•		H	Ø	Apr–Oct		14
8	Tajique			6			V			•	•	•	H	Ø	May–Oct		14

Hookups: W = Water   E = Electric   S = Sewer
Toilets: F = Flush   V = Vault   P = Pit   C = Chemical
Recreation: H = Hiking   S = Swimming   F = Fishing   B = Boating   L = Boat launch   O = Off-highway driving   R = Horseback riding
Maximum Trailer/RV Length given in feet.   **Stay Limit** given in days.   **Fee** $ = $0–5; $$ = $6–10; $$$ = $11–20.
If no entry under **Season,** campground is open all year. If no entry under **Fee,** camping is free.

1 Capilla Peak

Location: 12 miles west of Manzano
Sites: 8 sites for tents and RVs
Facilities: Vault toilets, tables, grills
Fee per night: $
Elevation: 9,200 feet
Management: Cibola National Forest, Mountainair Ranger District, 505-847-2990
Activities: Hiking, horseback riding
Finding the campground: From the town of Manzano on New Mexico 55, turn west onto Forest Road 245 and go 12 miles to the campground.

About the campground: Like other campgrounds in the Manzanos, Capilla Peak is primarily designed as a hiking access to the Manzano Wilderness. Trails lead right from camp. Capilla Peak is a bit less accessible than the other camps in the area, so if you're looking for a private hideout, this could be the place.

2 Fourth of July

Location: 33 miles south of Tijeras
Sites: 26 sites for tents and RVs
Facilities: Vault toilets, tables, grills, drinking water
Fee per night: $$
Elevation: 7,500 feet
Management: Cibola National Forest, Mountainair Ranger District,
505-847-2990
Activities: Hiking
Finding the campground: From I-40 in Tijeras, take exit 175. Go south 24 miles
on New Mexico Highway 337. Turn west onto NM 55 and go 2.5 miles to the town
of Tajique. Turn west onto Forest Road 55 and go 8 miles to the campground.

About the campground: Though it is somewhat difficult to get to, Fourth of
July is a popular spot, particularly for wildlife watching and hiking. Fall viewing
of Rocky Mountain maple leaves in full blazing color is another reason to in-
clude this camp on your itinerary, but the pines and oaks provide a lush retreat
throughout the year.

Sites are well spaced and all facilities were updated in 1997 and 1998. Hiking
trails into the Manzano Wilderness are near camp.

3 John F. Kennedy

Location: 25 miles east of Belen
Sites: 18 sites for tents and RVs
Facilities: Vault toilets, tables, grills, drinking water
Fee per night: $
Elevation: 6,300 feet
Management: Cibola National Forest, Mountainair Ranger District,
505-847-2990
Activities: Hiking, horseback riding
Finding the campground: In Belen, travel 2 miles east on New Mexico 309.
Turn south onto New Mexico 47 and go about 6 miles to County Road 68/Forest
Road 33. Turn east and go 17 miles to the campground.

About the campground: While the eastern side of the Manzano Mountains is
lush and green, the western slope is rugged desert with a beauty all its own. The
campground has nearby access to the Manzano Crest Trail for both hiking and
horseback riding.

4 Manzano Mountains State Park

Location: 13 miles northwest of Mountainair
Sites: 17 sites for tents and RVs
Facilities: Flush toilets, tables, grills, dump station, electricity, group site, trails
Fee per night: $ to $$, annual permit available
Elevation: 7,600 feet
Management: New Mexico State Parks Department, 505-847-2820, www.emnrd.state.nm.us/nmparks
Activities: Hiking, biking, horseback riding
Finding the campground: From Mountainair, travel north 10 miles on New Mexico Highway 55 to Manzano. Turn south onto New Mexico Highway 131 (which becomes Forest Road 253) and go about 3 miles to the park.

About the campground: If you're longing to enjoy a trek in the Manzanos but prefer a few creature comforts, this is the campground for you. The park offers the only electrical hookup sites and the only RV dump station in the region. All of the sites are well spaced among piñon and juniper trees, and the facilities are maintained in the typical state park fashion. The park also has its own set of trails in addition to nearby national forest trails into the Manzano Wilderness.

5 New Canyon

Location: 8 miles west of Manzano
Sites: 10 sites for tents and RVs
Facilities: Vault toilets, tables, grills, drinking water
Fee per night: $
Elevation: 7,800 feet
Management: Cibola National Forest, Mountainair Ranger District, 505-847-2990
Activities: Hiking
Finding the campground: From the town of Manzano on New Mexico 55, turn west onto Forest Road 245 and go 8 miles to the campground.

About the campground: This is hiker's heaven. The drawing card here is proximity to both the Manzano Crest Trail and the Osha Peak Trail. It would not be difficult to spend a full week exploring the Manzano Wilderness from this camp.

6 Red Canyon

Location: 15 miles northwest of Mountainair
Sites: 50 sites for tents and RVs
Facilities: Vault toilets, tables, grills, drinking water
Fee per night: $
Elevation: 8,000 feet
Management: Cibola National Forest, Mountainair Ranger District, 505-847-2990
Activities: Hiking, horseback riding
Finding the campground: From Mountainair travel north 10 miles on New Mexico Highway 55 to Manzano. Turn south onto New Mexico Highway 131 (which becomes Forest Road 253) and go about 4 miles to the campground.

About the campground: Load up the horses; this is the place to bring them. An entire section of this large, recently rebuilt campground is devoted to equestrian use. Corrals are located next to each campsite. Nearby Red Canyon and Spruce Canyon trails allow horseback traffic into the Manzano Wilderness.

Red Canyon is a lovely campground even if you don't have a horse. The pine trees tower over well-spaced sites with new and modern facilities. Overall, this is probably the nicest camp in the Manzanos.

7 Red Cloud

Location: 18 miles southwest of Corona
Sites: 4 sites for tents
Facilities: Vault toilets, tables, grills
Fee per night: None
Elevation: 7,900 feet
Management: Cibola National Forest, Mountainair Ranger District, 505-847-2990
Activities: Hiking, rock collecting
Finding the campground: From Corona, travel south 11 miles on U.S. Highway 54. Turn west onto Forest Road 161 and go 1 mile. Turn north onto Forest Road 99 and go 8 miles to the campground.

About the campground: Unless you are a hunter, a rockhound, or an old miner, you've probably never heard of Red Cloud. Located near an old mining district, this isolated camp is just the place if your intention is to escape the entire world. With only 4 developed sites you aren't likely to find any other occupants other than during deer hunting season. Bring a lounge chair and a few good books to read and you've got your own slice of heaven in the pines.

8 Tajique

Location: 30 miles south of Tijeras
Sites: 6 sites for tents
Facilities: Vault toilets, tables, grills
Fee per night: None
Elevation: 6,800 feet
Management: Cibola National Forest, Mountainair Ranger District, 505-847-2990
Activities: Hiking
Finding the campground: From I-40 in Tijeras, take exit 175. Go south 24 miles on New Mexico Highway 337. Turn west onto NM 55 and go 2.5 miles to the town of Tajique. Turn west onto Forest Road 55 and go 3 miles to the campground.

About the campground: If the reason you're camping in the Manzanos is to partake of all that Albuquerque has to offer, this is the best campground to choose. It has the easiest access to I-40 and isn't likely to be filled with hikers, who generally choose the higher camps first. It's not a bad place to hang your hat while enjoying one of the Southwest's finest cities.

Northeast

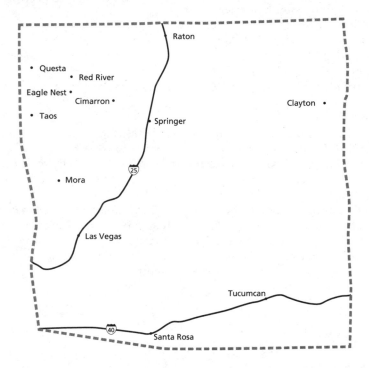

With resort towns like Taos, Red River, and Santa Fe, the northeast is the busy playground of the state. The campgrounds are often crowded, but the beauty of the Sangre de Cristos envelops you, drowning out the roar of the crowd. Crystal clear streams are plentiful and the wildlife is abundant.

Like most of the state, history is one of the top attractions here. The towns are rich with historical cultures—Spanish, Native American, and Mexican. Spend even a little time here and you'll begin to understand why New Mexico is called "The Land of Enchantment."

QUESTA–RED RIVER

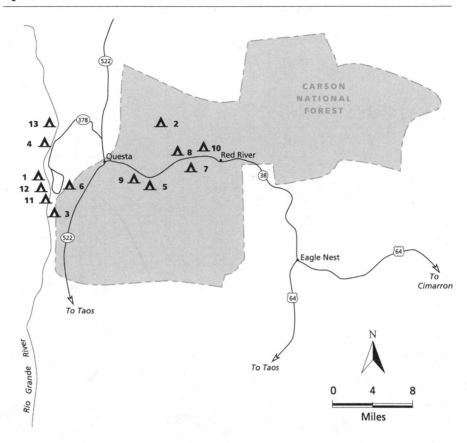

There are plenty of jokes about Texans and Red River. Most of them are funny; many of them are even true. But one saying that sums up the relationship best is "Ten thousand Texans can't be wrong." The two key points in that phrase are that on any given weekend you'll likely find Texans by the thousands in the area, and all of them have chosen one of the most enjoyable areas of the state to call their second home.

Red River and the surrounding area have good food, nightlife, family entertainment, Kodak scenery, trophy fly fishing, hiking to suit all fitness levels, and almost any other mountain activity you can think of. There are plenty of quiet spots to be found; they just aren't in the campgrounds.

Be advised that in recent years the Red River area has had a problem with frontcountry bears. As discussed in the introduction, these bears have lost their natural fear of man. They have come to prefer their dinners packed in an ice chest, so keep yours under lock and key. Follow all posted warnings and visit with rangers regarding any current warnings.

For more information:
Red River Chamber Of Commerce
P.O. Box 870
Red River, NM 87558
800-348-6444
www.redrivernewmex.com

Questa–Red River

		Group sites	RV sites	Total # of sites	Max. RV length	Hookups	Toilets	Showers	Drinking water	Dump station	Pets	Wheelchair	Recreation	Fee	Season	Can reserve	Stay limit
1	Big Arsenic Spring			D	22		V		•		•		HF	$$			14
2	Cabresto Lake			9			V				•		HF	$$	May–Sept		14
3	Cebolla Mesa			5			V		•		•		HF	$$			14
4	Chiflo			D	22		V		•		•		HF	$$			14
5	Columbine		•	27			V		•		•	•	HF	$$	May–Oct		14
6	El Aguaje		•	D	22		V		•		•		HF	$$			14
7	Elephant Rock		•	22			V		•		•	•	HF	$$	May–Oct		14
8	Fawn Lakes		•	22			V		•		•	•	HF	$$	May–Oct		14
9	Goat Hill			3			V				•		F	$$	May–Sept		14
10	Junebug		•	11			V		•		•		F	$$	May–Oct		14
11	La Junta			D	22		V		•		•	•	HF	$$			14
12	Little Arsenic Spring			D	22		V		•		•	•	HF	$$			14
13	Sheep Crossing			D	22		V		•		•	•	HF	$$			14

Hookups: W = Water E = Electric S = Sewer
Toilets: F = Flush V = Vault P = Pit C = Chemical
Recreation: H = Hiking S = Swimming F = Fishing B = Boating L = Boat launch O = Off-highway driving R = Horseback riding
Maximum Trailer/RV Length given in feet. **Stay Limit** given in days. **Fee** $ = $0–5; $$ = $6–10; $$$ = $11–20.
If no entry under **Season,** campground is open all year. If no entry under **Fee,** camping is free.

1 Big Arsenic Spring

Location: 10.5 miles southwest of Questa
Sites: Dispersed
Facilities: Vault toilets, tables, grills, drinking water
Fee per night: $$
Elevation: 6,500 feet
Management: Bureau of Land Management, 758-8851
Activities: Hiking, fishing, biking, whitewater sports
Finding the campground: From Questa, travel north 2 miles on New Mexico Highway 522. Turn west onto NM 378 and go 8.5 miles to the campground.

About the campground: This is one of seven developed campgrounds that make up the Bureau of Land Management's Wild Rivers Recreation Area. The area includes the confluence of the Red River and the Rio Grande and is a favorite for fly fishermen, hikers, and whitewater enthusiasts, as well as outdoor photographers and wildlife watchers.

The plunging 1000-foot cliffs that line the Rio Grande at the Rio Grande Gorge mark the southernmost point in the Wild Rivers Recreation Area, with the area extending north more than 20 miles. Camping at all of the campgrounds is on a first-come, first-served basis, but well worth the hassle of getting there early to secure a site.

2 Cabresto Lake

Location: 6 miles northeast of Questa
Sites: 9 sites for tents
Facilities: Vault toilets, tables, grills
Fee per night: $$
Elevation: 9,200 feet
Management: Carson National Forest, Questa Ranger District, 505-586-0520
Activities: Hiking, fishing
Finding the campground: From Questa, travel northeast 5 miles on Forest Road 134 to the campground access.

About the campground: Just try to describe the setting here without cliches. You can't talk about Cabresto Lake without using the words "breathtaking" or "serene." The only problem here is the road, which borders on being four-wheel drive. No trailers are allowed. If you get to Cabresto, attempt the 4-mile hike to Heart Lake, but go prepared because the cold will take you by surprise. Even a partial hike on this trail is worth the effort because the surroundings are so...um... okay, breathtaking.

3 Cebolla Mesa

Location: 13 miles southwest of Questa
Sites: 5 sites for tents
Facilities: Vault toilets, tables, grills, drinking water
Fee per night: $$
Elevation: 7,300 feet
Management: U.S. Bureau of Land Management, 505-758-8851
Activities: Hiking, fishing, biking
Finding the campground: From Questa, travel north 2 miles on New Mexico Highway 522. Turn west onto NM 378 and go 11 miles to the campground.

About the campground: Part of the Wild Rivers Recreation Area. See description at site1, Big Arsenic Spring.

The northern water of the Rio Grande has only a few calm places.

4 Chiflo

Location: 7.5 miles northwest of Questa
Sites: Dispersed
Facilities: Vault toilets, tables, grills, drinking water
Fee per night: $$
Elevation: 7,600 feet
Management: U.S. Bureau of Land Management, 505-758-8851
Activities: Hiking, fishing, biking, whitewater sports
Finding the campground: From Questa, travel north 2 miles on New Mexico Highway 522. Turn west onto NM 378 and go 5.5 miles to the campground.

About the campground: Part of the Wild Rivers Recreation Area. See description at site 1, Big Arsenic Spring.

5 Columbine

Location: 4.5 miles east of Questa
Sites: 27 sites for tents and RVs
Facilities: Vault toilets, tables, grills, drinking water
Fee per night: $$
Elevation: 7,900 feet
Management: Carson National Forest, Questa Ranger District, 505-586-0520
Activities: Hiking, fishing
Finding the campground: From Questa, travel 4.5 miles east on New Mexico Highway 38 to the campground.

About the campground: Besides being a lovely place from which to enjoy all the treats of the Red River area, Columbine provides access to the Columbine-Twinning Trail which crosses the Taos Mountains at more than 12,000 feet. Attempting the entire journey should be left up to serious hikers, but the rest of us can certainly enjoy a few miles up and back along this incredible trail.

6 El Aguaje

Location: 11 miles southwest of Questa
Sites: Dispersed
Facilities: Vault toilets, tables, grills, drinking water
Fee per night: $$
Elevation: 6,500 feet
Management: U.S. Bureau of Land Management, 505-758-8851
Activities: Hiking, fishing, biking, whitewater sports
Finding the campground: From Questa, travel north 2 miles on New Mexico Highway 522. Turn west onto NM 378 and go 9 miles to the campground.

About the campground: Part of the Wild Rivers Recreation Area. See description at site 1, Big Arsenic Spring.

7 Elephant Rock

Location: 3 miles west of Red River
Sites: 22 sites for tents and RVs
Facilities: Vault toilets, tables, grills, drinking water
Fee per night: $$
Elevation: 8,300 feet
Management: Carson National Forest, Questa Ranger District, 505-586-0520
Activities: Hiking, fishing
Finding the campground: From Red River, travel west 3 miles on New Mexico Highway 38 to the campground.

About the campground: As with the other roadside campgrounds along NM 38 between Red River and Questa, the main idea here is to have access to all those trout in the Red River and still be close enough to town to enjoy a night of dining and dancing. Elephant Rock fits the bill. Currently, none of the campgrounds on NM 38 are on the National Forest Reservation System, but it would not hurt to check. Call 877-444-6777.

8 Fawn Lakes

Location: 3.5 miles west of Red River
Sites: 22 sites for tents and RVs
Facilities: Vault toilets, tables, grills, drinking water
Fee per night: $$
Elevation: 8,500 feet
Management: Carson National Forest, Questa Ranger District, 505-586-0520
Activities: Hiking, fishing, biking
Finding the campground: From Red River, travel west 3.5 miles on New Mexico Highway 38 to the campground.

About the campground: Fawn Lakes is on the north side of NM 38 and provides fishing access to two stocked ponds. This makes it an ideal destination for those who prefer stillwater fishing over stream fishing. The campground was recently updated and the road paved, so you can expect modern facilities here.

9 Goat Hill

Location: 4 miles east of Questa
Sites: 3 sites for tents
Facilities: Vault toilets, tables, grills
Fee per night: $$
Elevation: 7,700 feet
Management: Carson National Forest, Questa Ranger District, 505-586-0520
Activities: Fishing
Finding the campground: From Questa, travel 4 miles east on New Mexico Highway 38 to the campground.

About the campground: If you can get a spot, this tiny camp is ideal for those looking to fish the Red River but who disdain the larger, busier campgrounds. The fact that it is the farthest camp from Red River also helps to thin the crowd. Give it a try during midweek, and you'll probably be alone.

10 Junebug

Location: 2 miles west of Red River
Sites: 11 sites for tents and RVs
Facilities: Vault toilets, tables, grills, drinking water
Fee per night: $$
Elevation: 8,500 feet
Management: Carson National Forest, Questa Ranger District, 505-586-0520
Activities: Fishing
Finding the campground: From Red River travel 2 miles west on New Mexico Highway 38 to the campground

About the campground: Junebug is as close to town as you can camp, so expect ten thousand Texans to be vying for these choice sites. If you can catch it either early or late in the season before the crowds hit, this is a pleasant little camp.

11 La Junta

Location: 12.5 miles southwest of Questa
Sites: Dispersed
Facilities: Vault toilets, tables, grills, drinking water
Fee per night: $$
Elevation: 6,500 feet
Management: U.S. Bureau of Land Management, 505-758-8851
Activities: Hiking, fishing, biking, whitewater sports
Finding the campground: From Questa travel north 2 miles on New Mexico Highway 522. Turn west onto NM 378 and go 10.5 miles to the campground.

About the campground: Part of the Wild Rivers Recreation Area. See description at site 1, Big Arsenic Spring.

12 Little Arsenic Spring

Location: 11 miles southwest of Questa
Sites: Dispersed
Facilities: Vault toilets, tables, grills, drinking water
Fee per night: $$
Elevation: 6,500 feet
Management: U.S. Bureau of Land Management, 505-758-8851
Activities: Hiking, fishing, biking, whitewater sports
Finding the campground: From Questa travel north 2 miles on New Mexico Highway 522. Turn west onto NM 378 and go 9.5 miles to the campground.

About the campground: Part of the Wild Rivers Recreation Area. See description at site 1, Big Arsenic Spring.

13 Sheep Crossing

Location: 6 miles northwest of Questa
Sites: Dispersed
Facilities: Vault toilets, tables, grills, drinking water
Fee per night: $$
Elevation: 6,500 feet
Management: U.S. Bureau of Land Management, 505-758-8851
Activities: Hiking, Fishing, biking, whitewater sports
Finding the campground: From Questa travel north 2 miles on New Mexico Highway 522. Turn west onto NM 378 and go 4 miles to the campground.

About the campground: Part of the Wild Rivers Recreation Area. See description at site 1, Big Arsenic Spring.

CIMARRON–EAGLE NEST

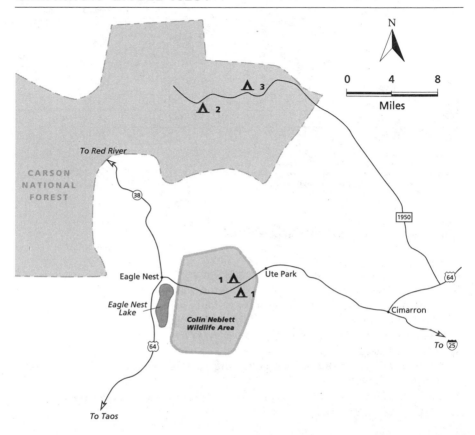

For many New Mexico visitors this area is practically a second home. The fishing at Eagle Nest Lake is ranked among the best in the state, the scenic drive through Cimarron Canyon is one you will not want to miss, and the hiking is ideal for all levels of trekkers. Rock collectors and geology buffs traverse the area known as the Palisades in search of agate and minerals, while wildlife enthusiasts are rarely disappointed in the abundance of flora and fauna found in the region.

Also, you are just around the bend from the bustling activity of Red River. The only drawback here is the crowded conditions. But if you don't mind bumping shoulders with fellow outdoor types, come on down.

For more information:

Cimarron Chamber of Commerce:
P.O. Box 604
Cimarron, NM 87714
505-376-2417

Eagle Nest Chamber of Commerce:
P.O. Box 322
Eagle Nest, NM 87718
505-377-2420

CIMARRON–EAGLE NEST

	Group sites	RV sites	Total # of sites	Max. RV length	Hookups	Toilets	Showers	Drinking water	Dump station	Pets	Wheelchair	Recreation	Fee	Season	Can reserve	Stay limit
1 Cimarron Canyon SP		•	100			V		•	•	•	•	HF	$-$$			14
2 Cimarron		•	32			V		•		•		HFR	$$	May–Nov		14
3 McCrystal		•	60			V		•		•	•	HFR	Ø	May–Oct		14

Hookups: W = Water E = Electric S = Sewer
Toilets: F = Flush V = Vault P = Pit C = Chemical
Recreation: H = Hiking S = Swimming F = Fishing B = Boating L = Boat launch O = Off-highway driving R = Horseback riding
Maximum Trailer/RV Length given in feet. **Stay Limit** given in days. **Fee** $ = $0–5; $$ = $6–10; $$$ = $11–20.
If no entry under **Season,** campground is open all year. If no entry under **Fee,** camping is free.

1 Cimarron Canyon State Park

Location: 7.5 miles east of Eagle Nest
Sites: 100 sites for tents and RVs, divided among 3 campgrounds
Facilities: Vault toilets, tables, grills, drinking water
Fee per night: $ to $$, annual permit available
Elevation: 8,000 feet
Management: New Mexico State Parks Department, 505-377-6271, www.emnrd.state.nm.us/nmparks
Activities: Hiking, fishing, rock collecting, scenic driving, biking, horseback riding
Finding the campground: From Eagle Nest, travel east 7.5 miles on U.S. Highway 64 to the campgrounds.

About the campground: Cimarron Canyon State Park is part of the Colin-Neblett Wildlife Area, the largest in the state and through which traverse trails suitable for hiking, biking, and horseback riding. The canyon itself presents a wealth of opportunities for exploring. Trailheads are found along U.S. 64 throughout the park, including two that take you up to the incredible Palisades rock formations.

There are two trailer campgrounds in the park, Maverick (formerly called Gravel Pit Lakes) and Ponderosa. Both are nice camps in Ponderosa pine forest, but with somewhat narrow spacing of sites. Keep in mind that these campgrounds fill quickly, so don't expect to pull in at midnight Friday and find a spot. Also, remember to practice bear-safe camping, because during most seasons the area has black furry visitors on a nightly basis.

2 Cimarron

Location: 40 miles northwest of Cimarron
Sites: 32 sites for tents and RVs
Facilities: Vault toilets, tables, grills, drinking water
Fee per night: $$
Elevation: 9,400 feet
Management: Carson National Forest, Questa Ranger District, 505-586-0520
Activities: Hiking, fishing, horseback riding
Finding the campground: From Cimarron, travel east 5.1 miles on U.S. Highway 64. Turn north onto Forest Road 1950 and go 35 miles to the campground.

About the campground: It's always odd to find such a large campground so far from everything. Cimarron and the neighboring McCrystal are popular, but not in the way the campgrounds in Cimarron Canyon are. The pace here is slower and the atmosphere quieter, probably because everyone who travels this far on a dirt road is serious about getting away from the rest of the world.

Fishing and additional unimproved sites are available on nearby Shuree Ponds, but the main attraction here besides the scenery is the elk. The Valle Vidal area of the Carson National Forest is known throughout the Southwest for its ever-increasing herd, so bring your binoculars.

3 McCrystal

Location: 35 miles northwest of Cimarron
Sites: 60 sites for tents and RVs
Facilities: Vault toilets, tables, grills, drinking water
Fee per night: None
Elevation: 8,100 feet
Management: Carson National Forest, Questa Ranger District, 505-586-0520
Activities: Hiking, fishing, horseback riding
Finding the campground: From Cimarron, travel east 5.1 miles on U.S. Highway 64. Turn north onto Forest Road 1950 and go 30 miles to the campground.

About the campground: McCrystal is another example of what a national forest campground can and should be: a place to retreat from the world into a setting that affords the opportunity to enjoy the grandeur of nature. Although there are 60 sites here, they are well spaced and, like neighboring Cimarron, most of your fellow campers here will be conscientious outdoors people.

CLAYTON–RATON–SPRINGER

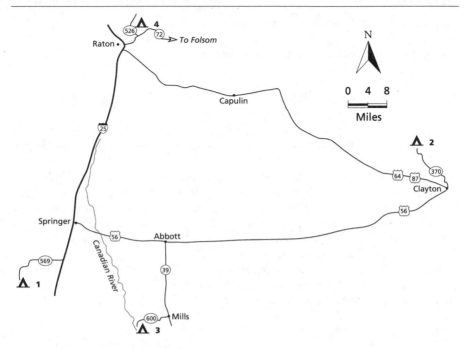

The northeastern corner of New Mexico is a prelude to the grander things to come as you near the Rocky Mountains. Massive volcanic craters jut from the plains, teasing the horizon. Desert mesas slowly give way to piñon-covered mountains. Though sparsely populated by humans, the triangle between Clayton, Raton and Springer is abundant with desert wildlife. Herds of pronghorn antelope sprint across the prairies in what is one of the few untouched areas of the Great Plains. People who pass through here are often too busy rushing north or west to appreciate the beauty, but those who slow down are well rewarded.

For more information:
Clayton/Union County Chamber of Commerce
P.O. Box 476
Clayton, NM 88415
505-374-9253

Raton Chamber of Commerce
P.O. Box 1211
Raton, NM 87740
505-445-3689
800-638-6161
www.raton.com/tourinfo.htm

Springer Chamber of Commerce
P.O. Box 607
Springer, NM 87747

CLAYTON–RATON–SPRINGER

		Group sites	RV sites	Total # of sites	Max. RV length	Hookups	Toilets	Showers	Drinking water	Dump station	Pets	Wheelchair	Recreation	Fee	Season	Can reserve	Stay limit
1	Charette Lakes			D			V				•		F	Ø	Mar–Oct		14
2	Clayton Lake State Park	•	•	33		WE	F	•	•	•	•	•	HFBL	$-$$			14
3	Mills Canyon			D			V						H	Ø			14
4	Sugarite Canyon State Park	•	•	40		E	F	•	•	•	•	•	HFBL	$-$$			14

Hookups: W = Water   E = Electric   S = Sewer
Toilets: F = Flush   V = Vault   P = Pit   C = Chemical
Recreation: H = Hiking   S = Swimming   F = Fishing   B = Boating   L = Boat launch   O = Off-highway driving   R = Horseback riding
Maximum Trailer/RV Length given in feet.   **Stay Limit** given in days.   **Fee** $ = $0–5; $$ = $6–10; $$$ = $11–20.
If no entry under **Season,** campground is open all year. If no entry under **Fee,** camping is free.

1 Charette Lakes Fishing Area

Location: 23 miles southwest of Springer
Sites: Dispersed
Facilities: Vault toilets, tables, boat ramp
Fee per night: None
Elevation: 5,800 feet
Management: New Mexico Game & Fish Department, 505-445-2311
Activities: Fishing, wildlife watching
Finding the campground: From Springer, travel 9 miles south on Interstate 25. Turn west onto New Mexico Highway 569 and go about 14 miles to the lakes.

About the campground: Perched in the shadow of Charette Mesa, these small lakes are a stopping place for thousands of migratory waterfowl, making it an unsurpassed spot for bird watchers. It also doesn't hurt that the lakes are periodically stocked with fish .

2 Clayton Lake State Park

Location: 15 miles northwest of Clayton
Sites: 33 sites for tents and RVs
Facilities: Flush toilets, showers, tables, grills, dump station, playground, boat launch, hiking trails
Fee per night: $ to $$, annual permit available
Elevation: 5,100 feet
Management: New Mexico State Parks Department, 505-374-8808, www.emnrd.state.nm.us/nmparks
Activities: Hiking, fishing, boating
Finding the campground: From Clayton, travel northwest 9 miles on New Mexico Highway 370. Turn west onto NM 455 and go 2 miles to the park.

About the campground: Besides the fishing and the lazy high-plains atmosphere, Clayton Lake offers a rare opportunity to view easily discernible dinosaur tracks captured in the mud of ancient watering holes. There are interpretive exhibits and a boardwalk which allows you to walk out over the track site. It's a fascinating adventure that makes a worthwhile side trip, even if you don't plan to camp here.

The campground has the comforts of most New Mexico state parks.

3 Mills Canyon

Location: 42 miles southeast of Springer
Sites: Dispersed, tents only
Facilities: Vault toilets
Fee per night: None
Elevation: 5,100 feet
Management: Kiowa National Grasslands, 505-374-9652
Activities: Hiking, wildlife watching
Finding the campground: From Springer, travel 18 miles east on U.S. Highway 56 to Abbott. Turn south onto New Mexico Highway 39 and go 16.5 miles. Turn west onto County Road U1 (which becomes Forest Road 600) and go 8 miles to the canyon.

About the campground: This is primitive camping at its finest in lowland New Mexico. Tent camping is possible at the canyon rim, but the choice spots are at the end of a two-mile trail that drops the last 800 feet into the canyon. The road getting here is bad when dry and impassible when wet. High-clearance vehicles are recommended. This campground serves as a reminder that the good things in life are always at the end of the roughest roads.

4 Sugarite Canyon State Park

Location: 10 miles northeast of Raton
Sites: 40 sites for tents and RVs
Facilities: Flush toilets, visitor center, group sites, electricity, tables, grills, drinking water, dump station, showers, hiking trails, boat launch
Fee per night: $ to $$, annual permit available
Elevation: 7,800 feet
Management: New Mexico State Parks Department, 505-445-5607, www.emnrd.state.nm.us/nmparks
Activities: Hiking, fishing, boating, scenic driving
Finding the campground: From Interstate 25, take exit 452 in Raton. Turn east onto New Mexico Highway 72 and go 3 miles. Turn north onto NM 526 and go 2 miles to the park.

About the campground: Sugarite is a world all its own, tucked away in the hills outside Raton. Few other than New Mexican locals even know it exists. The setting includes pine-covered hillsides and rolling mountain meadows. If you can include this park in your New Mexico itinerary, you won't be disappointed.

TUCUMCARI

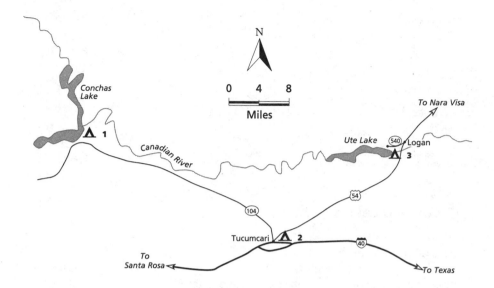

Curled beneath the colorful mesa known as Tucumcari Mountain, this New Mexico gateway city still thrives on the memory of U.S. Route 66. The town is quaint and has all the conveniences. And, some of the state's best water sports areas are just a stone's throw away.

For more information:
Tucumcari-Quay County Chamber of Commerce
404 W. Tucumcari Boulevard
P.O. Drawer E
Tucumcari, NM 88401
505-461-1694
www.tucumcarinm.com

TUCUMCARI

	Group sites	RV sites	Total # of sites	Max. RV length	Hookups	Toilets	Showers	Drinking water	Dump station	Pets	Wheelchair	Recreation	Fee	Season	Can reserve	Stay limit
1 Conchas Lake State Park	•	•	101		WE	F	•	•	•	•	•	HFBL	$-$$			14
2 Tucumcari SWA	•	•	D			V						F	Ø			14
3 Ute Lake State Park	•	•	98		WE	F	•	•	•	•	•	HFBL	$-$$			14

Hookups: W = Water   E = Electric   S = Sewer
Toilets: F = Flush   V = Vault   P = Pit   C = Chemical
Recreation: H = Hiking   S = Swimming   F = Fishing   B = Boating   L = Boat launch   O = Off-highway driving   R = Horseback riding
Maximum Trailer/RV Length given in feet. **Stay Limit** given in days. **Fee** $ = $0–5; $$ = $6–10; $$$ = $11–20.
If no entry under **Season,** campground is open all year. If no entry under **Fee,** camping is free.

1 Conchas Lake State Park

Location: 34 miles northwest of Tucumcari
Sites: 101 sites for tents and RVs
Facilities: Flush toilets, visitor center, electricity, dump station, tables, grills, drinking water, showers, marina, playground, hiking trails, boat launch, shelters, golf course
Fee per night: $ to $$, annual permit available
Elevation: 4,200 feet
Management: New Mexico State Parks Department, 505-868-2270, www.emnrd.state.nm.us/nmparks
Activities: Hiking, fishing, water sports, scuba diving
Finding the campground: From Tucumcari, travel 34 miles northwest on New Mexico Highway 104 to the park.

About the campground: This is the desert Southwest, so don't expect to use the words "lush" or "green" to describe Conchas. "Colorful" does apply, however. The earth is red and the sky and water are clear blue. The water is clear enough, in fact, to attract scuba divers almost year-round. It isn't the Caribbean, but treasure hunting is a popular pastime among the divers.

The campgrounds are well maintained, with plenty of space between sites and plenty of parking for boats. As at any body of water in New Mexico, expect crowds during the busy summer season.

▌ Tucumcari State Wildlife Area

Location: 1 mile east of Tucumcari
Sites: Dispersed
Facilities: Vault toilets
Fee per night: None
Elevation: 4,300 feet
Management: New Mexico Game & Fish Department, Northeast Office, 505-445-2311
Activities: Fishing, wildlife watching
Finding the campground: From Tucumcari, travel east 1 mile on U.S. Highway 54 to the park entrance.

About the campground: If you just want to fish, this is one possible place to get away from the water sports crowd that has taken over Conchas. Formerly known as the Ladd S. Gordon State Wildlife Area, this area is home to the 400-acre Tucumcari Lake. Boats are allowed, but only with electric motors. Fishing is variable, but the scenery is always top quality.

▌ Ute Lake State Park

Location: 3 miles west of Logan
Sites: 98 sites for tents and RVs
Facilities: Flush toilets, tables, grills, drinking water, visitor center, group sites, electricity, dump station, showers, marina, hiking trails
Fee per night: $ to $$, annual permit available
Elevation: 3,900 feet
Management: New Mexico State Parks Department, 505-487-2284, www.emnrd.state.nm.us/nmparks
Activities: Hiking, fishing, boating
Finding the campground: From Logan, travel 3 miles west on New Mexico Highway 540 to the park.

About the campground: Though considerably smaller than its neighbor Conchas, Ute Lake is popular among bass anglers throughout New Mexico and parts of Texas. The campground is nestled along the shore, with some shade provided by cottonwoods. Expect crowds almost anytime of year.

TAOS–PILAR

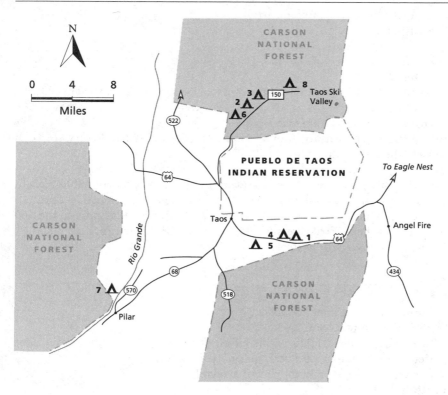

Art, fashion, food, whitewater rafting, and jagged mountain peaks—if you're going to New Mexico in search of anything else, then don't bother with Taos. Save it for the rest of us who thrive on the magic of this place. For over a hundred years artists and writers have drifted to Taos, and their influence is unmistakable in the city and surrounding area. The mountains near Taos are a work of art in themselves, supplying the best skiing in the state in winter and some of the best climbing and hiking during the rest of the year.

For more information:
Taos County Chamber of Commerce
P.O. Drawer I
Taos, New Mexico 87571
800-732-TAOS (8267)
www.taoschamber.com

TAOS–PILAR

	Group sites	RV sites	Total # of sites	Max. RV length	Hookups	Toilets	Showers	Drinking water	Dump station	Pets	Wheelchair	Recreation	Fee	Season	Can reserve	Stay limit
1 Capulin		•	10	16		V		•		•	•	HF	$$	May–Oct		14
2 Cuchillo de Medio		•	3	16		V				•		F	Ø	May–Sept		14
3 Italianos		•	3	16		V				•		HF	$$	May–Oct		14
4 La Sombra		•	13	16		V		•		•	•	HF	$$	May–Oct		14
5 Las Petacas		•	9			V				•		F	$$	Apr–Nov		14
6 Lower Hondo		•	4	16		V				•		F	$$	May–Sept		14
7 Orilla Verde NRA	•		23			V		•		•	•	HF	$$			14
8 Twining		•	4	16		V				•		FH	$$	May–Sept		14

Hookups: W = Water E = Electric S = Sewer
Toilets: F = Flush V = Vault P = Pit C = Chemical
Recreation: H = Hiking S = Swimming F = Fishing B = Boating L = Boat launch O = Off-highway driving R = Horseback riding
Maximum Trailer/RV Length given in feet. **Stay Limit** given in days. **Fee** $ = $0–5; $$ = $6–10; $$$ = $11–20.
If no entry under **Season,** campground is open all year. If no entry under **Fee,** camping is free.

1 Capulin

Location: 6 miles east of Taos
Sites: 10 sites for tents and RVs
Facilities: Vault toilets, tables, grills, drinking water
Fee per night: $$
Elevation: 8,000 feet
Management: Carson National Forest, Camino Real District, 505-587-2255
Activities: Hiking, fishing
Finding the campground: From Taos, travel east 6 miles on U.S. Highway 64 to the campground.

About the campground: Capulin is a pleasant little roadside campground between Taos and Angel Fire. It's a good spot from which to explore the Taos area but will work just as well if you're inclined only to pull out the lawn chairs and do nothing. There's a strail to the nearby Ice Cave waterfall for a bit of added interest. The campground fills quickly.

2 Cuchillo de Medio

Location: 13 miles northeast of Taos
Sites: 3 sites for tents and RVs
Facilities: Vault toilets, tables, grills
Fee per night: None
Elevation: 7,800 feet
Management: Carson National Forest, Canjilon Ranger District, 505-684-2486
Activities: Fishing
Finding the campground: From Taos, travel northwest 3 miles on New Mexico Highway 522. Turn north on NM 230 and go 2.5 miles to NM 150. Turn east and go 7.5 miles to the campground.

About the campground: This is one of four opportunities to camp along the Rio Hondo on the road to the Taos Ski Valley. The problem is that all four camps are tiny, so if this is where you want to be, you'd better get here midweek. The scenery is spectacular and the fishing usually good. Although the campground is small, it's not an ideal spot to escape fellow travelers due to the potential for road noise.

3 Italianos

Location: 16 miles northeast of Taos
Sites: 3 sites for tents and RVs
Facilities: Vault toilets, tables, grills
Fee per night: $$
Elevation: 7,800 feet
Management: Carson National Forest, Canjilon Ranger District, 505-684-2486
Activities: Hiking, fishing
Finding the campground: From Taos travel northwest 3 miles on New Mexico Highway 522. Turn north on NM 230 and go 2.5 miles to NM 150. Turn east and go 9.5 miles to the campground.

About the campground: Hikers will appreciate this small camp for its easy access to the Wheeler Peak Wilderness Area. Everybody else will appreciate it for sheer beauty. It's nice to find camping right off pavement, but don't forget the potential for road noise, especially on weekends.

4 La Sombra

Location: 6 miles east of Taos
Sites: 13 sites for tents and RVs
Facilities: Vault toilets, tables, grills, drinking water
Fee per night: $$
Elevation: 7,800 feet
Management: Carson National Forest, Camino Real Ranger District, 505-587-2255
Activities: Hiking, fishing
Finding the campground: From Taos, travel east 6 miles on U.S. Highway 64 to the campground.

About the campground: Camping in Taos Canyon is heaven for those who like convenience to stores, a place to fish, and perfect New Mexican scenery. Keep in mind that everybody else wants a slice of heaven, too, so you have to arrive early to get one of these 13 sites.

5 Las Petacas

Location: 4 miles east of Taos
Sites: 9 sites for tents and RVs
Facilities: Vault toilets, tables, grills
Fee per night: $$
Elevation: 7,400 feet
Management: Carson National Forest, Camino Real Ranger District, 505-587-2255
Activities: Fishing
Finding the campground: From Taos, travel east 4 miles on U.S. Highway 64 to the campground.

About the campground: Las Petacas is the closest public campground to Taos. The pines and cottonwoods of Taos Canyon blend into a shimmering sea of green that begs you to never leave, so bring a hammock and plan to stay awhile.

6 Lower Hondo

Location: 11.5 miles northeast of Taos
Sites: 4 sites for tents and RVs
Facilities: Vault toilets, tables, grills
Fee per night: $$
Elevation: 7,700 feet
Management: Carson National Forest, Camino Real Ranger District, 505-587-2255
Activities: Fishing
Finding the campground: From Taos, travel northwest 3 miles on New Mexico Highway 522. Turn north on New Mexico 230 and go 2.5 miles to New Mexico 150. Turn east and go 6.5 miles to the campground.

About the campground: Lower Hondo is the lowest among the string of campgrounds on the Rio Hondo. Primary use is by hikers seeking proximity to the Wheeler Peak Wilderness Area, which borders NM 150. The four sites here make a very nice retreat, if you can find one available.

7 Orilla Verde National Recreation Area

Location: 2 miles north of Pilar
Sites: 23 sites for tents
Facilities: Vault toilets, tables, grills, drinking water, group sites
Fee per night: $$
Elevation: 6,000 feet
Management: Bureau of Land Management, 505-758-8851
Activities: Hiking, fishing
Finding the campground: From Pilar, travel north 2 miles on New Mexico Highway 570 to the campground.

About the campground: As part of the U.S. Bureau of Land Management's Wild and Scenic River Project, Orilla provides access to the rushing waters of the Rio Grande. Whitewater sports are the big draw here, but fly fishing is also a popular pastime. If you're willing to come down from campgrounds in the mountains these campsites along the river are a real treat.

8 Twining

Location: 19 miles northeast of Taos
Sites: 4 sites for tents and RVs
Facilities: Vault toilets, tables, grills
Fee per night: $$
Elevation: 9,300 feet
Management: Carson National Forest, Camino Real Ranger District, 505-587-2255
Activities: Fishing, hiking
Finding the campground: From Taos travel northwest 3 miles on New Mexico Highway 522. Turn north on NM 230 and go 2.5 miles to NM 150. Turn east and go 12.5 miles to the campground.

About the campground: What would camping near Taos be without the opportunity to experience Wheeler Peak? These four sites at Twining offer the high-country experience at its finest. From here you can hike to your heart's content, then come back to the comfort of your trailer to relive the day's adventure. Just keep in mind that like all campsites near Taos, these are first-come-first-served, so be early.

TRES RITOS

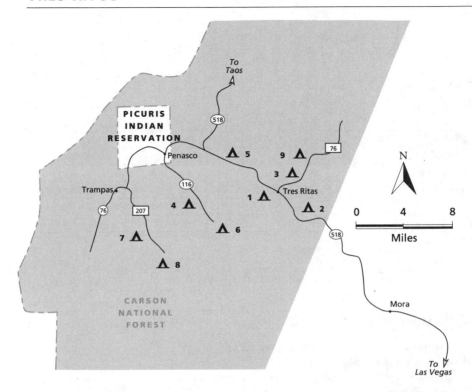

Ask any Texan who camps in New Mexico and they will be happy to tell you all about Tres Ritos. Unlike other spots that have been more recently "discovered" by campers, Tres Ritos has been a favorite for decades. Located deep in the heart of the Sangre de Cristo Mountains, this is the place to escape the traffic noise, the phones, and the rush of the world. Unfortunately, you won't escape the crowd, but there's usually plenty of space for everyone. Fishing is good in several streams and rivers that course through the area, and trail activities like hiking, horseback riding, and mountain biking are all possible from here.

TRES RITOS

	Group sites	RV sites	Total # of sites	Max. RV length	Hookups	Toilets	Showers	Drinking water	Dump station	Pets	Wheelchair	Recreation	Fee	Season	Can reserve	Stay limit
1 Agua Piedra	•	•	13	32		V		•		•	•	HFR	$$	May–Oct		14
2 Angostura			11			V				•		HF	$$	May–Sept		14
3 Duran Canyon		•	12			V		•		•		HFR	$$	May–Sept	•	14
4 Hodges			14			V				•		HFR	$	May–Oct		14
5 Llanito Frio		•	14			V				•		F	$$	May–Oct		14
6 Santa Barbara		•	12			V		•		•		HFR	$$	May–Sept		14
7 Trampas Diamante		•	5	16		V				•		HR	$	May–Sept		14
8 Trampas Trailhead			5			V				•		HR	Ø	May–Sept		14
9 Upper La Junta		•	8	16		V				•		HF	$	May–Oct		14

Hookups: W = Water E = Electric S = Sewer
Toilets: F = Flush V = Vault P = Pit C = Chemical
Recreation: H = Hiking S = Swimming F = Fishing B = Boating L = Boat launch O = Off-highway driving R = Horseback riding
Maximum Trailer/RV Length given in feet. **Stay Limit** given in days. **Fee** $ = $0–5; $$ = $6–10; $$$ = $11–20.
If no entry under **Season,** campground is open all year. If no entry under **Fee,** camping is free.

1 Agua Piedra

Location: 1.5 miles northwest of Tres Ritos
Sites: 13 sites for tents and RVs
Facilities: Vault toilets, tables, grills, drinking water
Fee per night: $$
Elevation: 8,400 feet
Management: Carson National Forest, Camino Real Ranger District, 505-587-2255
Activities: Hiking, fishing, horseback riding
Finding the campground: From Tres Ritos, travel 1.5 miles northwest on New Mexico Highway 518 to the campground.

About the campground: One of the easily accessible campgrounds along New Mexico Highway 518, Agua Piedra offers fishing access to the Rio Pueblo. The sites are well spaced among the pines, and three additional primitive sites are located nearby at South Agua Piedra. Bring a hammock because this place is comfortable. Remember that because it's on the main road, it is more likely to fill quickly.

2 Angostura

Location: 2 miles southeast of Tres Ritos
Sites: 11 sites for tents
Facilities: Vault toilets, tables, grills
Fee per night: $$
Elevation: 8,800 feet
Management: Carson National Forest, Camino Real Ranger District, 505-587-2255
Activities: Hiking, fishing
Finding the campground: From Tres Ritos travel 2 miles southeast on New Mexico Highway 518 to the campground.

About the campground: Located between the towns of Tres Ritos and Angostura, this medium-sized camp is a popular one among anglers. The pine trees and Rio Pueblo beg you to spend an extra couple of days here, so plan accordingly.

3 Duran Canyon

Location: 2 miles northeast of Tres Ritos
Sites: 12 sites for tents and RVs
Facilities: Vault toilets, tables, grills, drinking water
Fee per night: $$
Elevation: 9,000 feet
Management: Carson National Forest, Camino Real Ranger District, 505-587-2255
Reservations: 877-444-6777, www.reserveusa.com, $8.65 fee
Activities: Hiking, fishing, horseback riding
Finding the campground: From Tres Ritos, travel 2 miles northeast on New Mexico Highway 76 to the campground.

About the campground: Duran Canyon is the only camp in the Tres Ritos area with reservable sites, and they are limited in number. Reservations can be made as early as 240 days in advance, so it's not a bad idea to plan well ahead of schedule to ensure sites.

4 Hodges

Location: 6 miles southeast of Penasco
Sites: 14 sites for tents
Facilities: Vault toilets, tables, grills
Fee per night: $
Elevation: 8,000 feet
Management: Carson National Forest, Camino Real Ranger District, 505-587-2255
Activities: Hiking, fishing, horseback riding
Finding the campground: From Penasco, travel 6 miles southeast on Forest Road 116 to the campground.

About the campground: Hodges sometimes serves as an overflow area for the more popular Santa Barbara campground farther down the road, but there's no reason not to make this your intended destination. The surroundings are peaceful, the campground well laid out, and it's a bit more off the beaten track than those closer to Tres Ritos.

5 Llanito Frio

Location: 6 miles west of Tres Ritos
Sites: 14 sites for tents and RVs
Facilities: Vault toilets, tables, grills
Fee per night: $$
Elevation: 7,800 feet
Management: Carson National Forest, Camino Real Ranger District, 505-587-2255
Activities: Fishing
Finding the campground: From Tres Ritos, travel 6 miles west on New Mexico Highway 518 to the campground.

About the campground: This is another mid-sized camp along New Mexico 518, making it easily accessible for larger trailers. Like the other camps in the area, this one will be full if you try to pull in at midnight on Friday, so plan accordingly.

The Santa Barbara River flows near the Tres Ritos-area campsites.

6 Santa Barbara

Location: 9 miles southeast of Penasco
Sites: 12 sites for tents and RVs
Facilities: Vault toilets, tables, grills, drinking water
Fee per night: $$
Elevation: 8,800 feet
Management: Carson National Forest, Camino Real Ranger District, 505-587-2255
Activities: Hiking, fishing, horseback riding
Finding the campground: From Penasco, travel 9 miles southeast on Forest Road 116 to the campground.

About the campground: Santa Barbara is the largest and probably the most popular campground in the Tres Ritos area. With access to the trails leading into the Pecos Wilderness, many use it as a drop-off point for hiking the Truchas-area peaks. Horse corrals are available for trail riders as well.

7 Trampas Diamante

Location: 7 miles southeast of Trampas
Sites: 5 sites for tents and RVs
Facilities: Vault toilets, tables, grills
Fee per night: $
Elevation: 8,900 feet
Management: Carson National Forest, Camino Real Ranger District, 505-587-2255
Activities: Hiking, horseback riding
Finding the campground: From Trampas, travel 1 mile north on New Mexico Highway 76. Turn southeast onto Forest Road 207 and go 6 miles to the campground.

About the campground: These primitive sites offer something you aren't likely to find elsewhere in the Tres Ritos area: solitude. The road keeps many away; the lack of fishing access keeps the rest away. If you want to enjoy the peace and quiet and perhaps hike the Trampas Peak, this is the place.

8 Trampas Trailhead

Location: 10 miles southeast of Trampas
Sites: 5 sites for tents
Facilities: Vault toilets, tables, grills
Fee per night: None
Elevation: 9,000 feet
Management: Carson National Forest, Camino Real Ranger District, 505-587-2255
Activities: Hiking, horseback riding
Finding the campground: From Trampas, travel 1 mile north on New Mexico Highway 76. Turn southeast onto Forest Road 207 and go 9 miles to the campground.

About the campground: Here's a level of camping that falls somewhere between the cozy comforts of RVing and true, rough, off-road camping. If that in-between level is what you seek, try this small camp. With only five sites, you can expect little in the way of company other than the squirrels and hummingbirds. This is what camping in New Mexico used to be like—no rush, no crowds.

9 Upper La Junta

Location: 4 miles northeast of Tres Ritos
Sites: 8 sites for tents and RVs
Facilities: Vault toilets, tables, grills
Fee per night: $
Elevation: 9,000 feet
Management: Carson National Forest, Camino Real Ranger District, 505-587-2255
Activities: Hiking, fishing, mountain biking
Finding the campground: From Tres Ritos, travel 4 miles northeast on Forest Road 76 to the campground.

About the campground: The crowds are a bit thinner here than along the highway below. Fishing access to the Rio La Junta provides plenty of opportunity to catch a trout or two. The camp is also a popular base camp for mountain bikers and dirt bikers (both of which are allowed on nearby trails).

LAS VEGAS–MORA

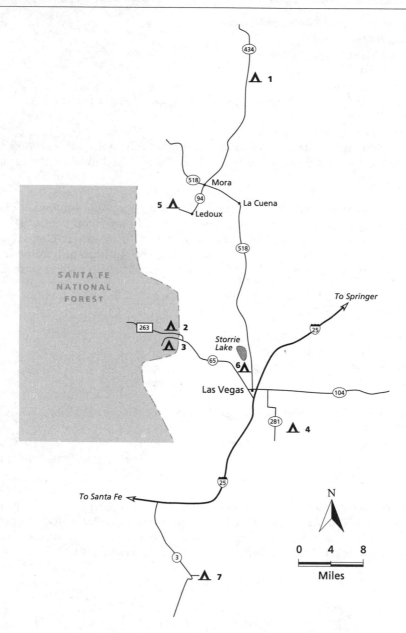

Billed as the gateway between the Great Plains and the Rocky Mountains, Las Vegas is an interesting mix of genuine New Mexican culture and tourist glitz. You won't find as much artiness here, nor as many tourists, as in Santa Fe or Taos. This works to your advantage if you're looking for someplace a bit quieter. The mountains west of here are every bit as beautiful as those deeper in the heart of the state, so you won't be disappointed in these campgrounds.

For more information:
Las Vegas/San Miguel County Chamber of Commerce
P.O. Box 148
Las Vegas, NM 87701
www.lasvegasnewmexico.com/Las.Vegas.New.Mexico/chamber.htm

LAS VEGAS–MORA

	Group sites	RV sites	Total # of sites	Max. RV length	Hookups	Toilets	Showers	Drinking water	Dump station	Pets	Wheelchair	Recreation	Fee	Season	Can reserve	Stay limit
1 Coyote Creek SP	•	•	20		WE	F	•	•	•	•	•	HF	$-$$			14
2 El Porvenir		•	19			V	•			•	•	HFR	$$	May–Oct		14
3 E. V. Long			21	16		V	•			•		F	$$	May–Oct		14
4 McAlister Lake			D			V					•	F	Ø			14
5 Morphy Lake State Park			D			V					•	F	$-$$			14
6 Storrie Lake State Park	•	•	37		WE	F	•	•	•	•	•	HFB	$-$$			14
7 Villanueva State Park	•	•	28		WE	F	•	•	•	•	•	HF	$-$$			14

Hookups: W = Water   E = Electric   S = Sewer
Toilets: F = Flush   V = Vault   P = Pit   C = Chemical
Recreation: H = Hiking   S = Swimming   F = Fishing   B = Boating   L = Boat launch   O = Off-highway driving   R = Horseback riding
Maximum Trailer/RV Length given in feet.   **Stay Limit** given in days.   **Fee** $ = $0–5; $$ = $6–10; $$$ = $11–20.
If no entry under **Season**, campground is open all year. If no entry under **Fee**, camping is free.

---

1 Coyote Creek State Park

Location: 16 miles north of Mora
Sites: 20 sites for tents and RVs
Facilities: Flush toilets, tables, grills, drinking water, visitor center, group sites, electricity, dump station, showers, playground, hiking trails
Fee per night: $ to $$, annual permit available
Elevation: 7,700 feet
Management: New Mexico State Parks Department, 505-387-2328, www.emnrd.state.nm.us/nmparks
Activities: Hiking, fishing
Finding the campground: From Mora, travel 16 miles north on New Mexico Highway 434 to the campground.

About the campground: Coyote Creek is a pleasant place to camp if you enjoy viewing the mountains from a distance. It also makes a nice stopover on your way deeper into the Rockies. All the usual state park amenities are here, scattered amid a light spruce forest. Easy hiking trails lead through the forest and fishing is excellent in Coyote Creek and the beaver ponds along it.

2 El Porvenir

Location: 16 miles northwest of Las Vegas
Sites: 19 sites for tents and RVs
Facilities: Vault toilets, tables, grills, drinking water
Fee per night: $$
Elevation: 7,600 feet
Management: Santa Fe National Forest, 505-425-3534
Activities: Hiking, fishing, horseback riding
Finding the campground: From Las Vegas, travel northwest 16 miles on New Mexico Highway 65 to the campground.

About the campground: It's hard to find a campground on the eastern slope of the Rockies that qualifies as unpopular. And, while El Porvenir is far from unpopular, it is at least a bit less popular than spots farther into the mountains. That isn't to say that this camp is any less attractive, though. The pines are dense and fishing is possible in Gallinas Creek. Also, the trail to Hermit's Peak is nearby.

3 E.V. Long

Location: 18 miles northwest of Las Vegas
Sites: 21 sites for tents and RVs
Facilities: Vault toilets, tables, grills, drinking water
Fee per night: $$
Elevation: 7,500 feet
Management: Santa Fe National Forest, 505-425-3534
Activities: Fishing
Finding the campground: From Las Vegas, travel northwest 16 miles on New Mexico Highway 65. Turn onto Forest Road 263 and go 1 mile to the campground.

About the campground: Like its neighbor El Porvenir, this camp is just a fraction less popular than many camps farther north and west, but you can still expect both of them to fill on most summer weekends. Try either of them on weekdays if you're looking for solitude.

4 McAlister Lake

Location: 7 miles southeast of Las Vegas
Sites: Dispersed
Facilities: Vault toilets
Fee per night: None
Management: New Mexico Department of Game and Fish, 505-827-7882
Activities: Fishing
Finding the campground: From Interstate 25, take exit 345 and travel east 1 mile on New Mexico Highway 104. Turn south onto New Mexico 281 and go 7 miles to the lake.

About the campground: This New Mexico Department of Game & Fish lake is well worth the stop if you like wide-open spaces and lake fishing. The lake is stocked and if you yearn for the smell of pines the mountains are just a short drive away.

5 Morphy Lake State Park

Location: 11 miles southwest of Mora
Sites: Dispersed
Facilities: Vault toilets, tables, grills
Fee per night: $ to $$, annual permit available
Elevation: 7,800 feet
Management: New Mexico State Parks Department, 505-387-2328, www.emnrd.state.nm.us/nmparks
Activities: Fishing
Finding the campground: From Mora, travel south 6 miles on New Mexico Highway 94. Turn west onto Forest Road 635 and go 3 miles to the park.

About the campground: Morphy Lake isn't a typical state park campground. Not only does a very rough, steep road limit access, but there are no developed sites. The lake is Kodak-perfect, with a rocky shoreline surrounded by dense pines. You may actually be able to break away from the crowds at Morphy, but if you drive anything but a four-wheel drive vehicle, call ahead for road conditions.

6 Storrie Lake State Park

Location: 4 miles north of Las Vegas
Sites: 37 sites for tents and RVs
Facilities: Flush toilets, tables, grills, drinking water, visitor center, group sites, electricity, dump station, showers, playground
Fee per night: $ to $$, annual permit available
Elevation: 6,400 feet
Management: New Mexico State Parks Department, 505-425-7278, www.emnrd.state.nm.us/nmparks
Activities: Hiking, fishing, boating, waterskiing, sailing, windsurfing, scenic driving
Finding the campground: From Las Vegas, travel 5 miles north on New Mexico Highway 518 to the campground.

About the campground: Like Las Vegas itself, Storrie Lake presents a nice gateway to the mountains. You can sit on the shore watching your line and find yourself mesmerized by the beauty of the not-too-distant peaks of the Sangre de Cristos. If a bit more activity is your style, bring a windsurfer (and a wetsuit) and give the breezes here a whirl.

7 Villanueva State Park

Location: 31 miles southwest of Las Vegas
Sites: 28 for tents and RVs
Facilities: Flush toilets, tables, grills, drinking water, visitor center, group sites, electricity, dump station, showers, playground, hiking trails
Fee per night: $ to $$, annual permit available
Elevation: 5,600 feet
Management: New Mexico State Parks Department, 505-421-2957, www.emnrd.state.nm.us/nmparks
Activities: Hiking, fishing
Finding the campground: From I-25 south of Las Vegas, take exit 323 and travel south on New Mexico Highway 3 to the park.

About the campground: Villanueva is for lovers of the Southwest lifestyle. There are historic ruins to hike to, the campsites are designed to resemble a native village, and the whole park is situated amid red sandstone bluffs on the banks of the Pecos River. The setting is picturesque but don't come looking for mountain scenery and pine trees.

PECOS

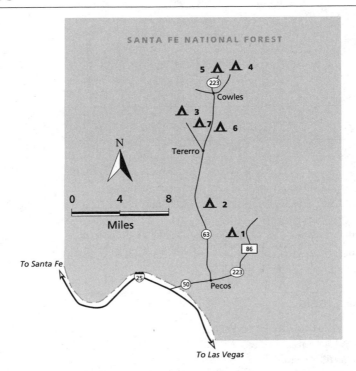

The mountains north of the town of Pecos have always been a popular destination, but ever-increasing numbers of campers are discovering the rugged beauty found here. The attraction lies in the easy access to the Pecos Wilderness plus the trophy-quality fishing in the Pecos River. Some campgrounds are designated as equestrian camps, and the area is especially popular with trail riders.

The region has a history in mining and draws students of geology to the red walled canyons leading into the mountains. Amateur rock collectors also come looking for slivers of mineral treasure left behind by the miners.

Most people, though, come just for the smell of the pine trees and the whisper of the wind.

PECOS

	Group sites	RV sites	Total # of sites	Max. RV length	Hookups	Toilets	Showers	Drinking water	Dump station	Pets	Wheelchair	Recreation	Fee	Season	Can reserve	Stay limit
1 Cow Creek			5			V				•		F	Ø	May–Oct		14
2 Field Tract		•	20			V		•		•		HF	$$	May–Oct		14
3 Holy Ghost	•	•	24	32		V		•		•	•	HF	$$	May–Oct	•	14
4 Iron Gate		•	14	16		V				•		HR	Ø	May–Oct		14
5 Jack's Creek	•	•	39	16		V		•		•		HFR	$$	May–Oct		14
6 Mora River			D			V						HF	Ø			14
7 Willow Creek		•	20	17		V				•		HF	Ø	Apr–Nov		14

Hookups: W = Water E = Electric S = Sewer
Toilets: F = Flush V = Vault P = Pit C = Chemical
Recreation: H = Hiking S = Swimming F = Fishing B = Boating L = Boat launch O = Off-highway driving R = Horseback riding
Maximum Trailer/RV Length given in feet. **Stay Limit** given in days. **Fee** $ = $0–5; $$ = $6–10; $$$ = $11–20.
If no entry under **Season**, campground is open all year. If no entry under **Fee**, camping is free.

1 Cow Creek

Location: 8 miles northeast of Pecos
Sites: 5 sites for tents
Facilities: Vault toilets, tables, grills
Fee per night: None
Elevation: 8,200 feet
Management: Santa Fe National Forest, Pecos/Las Vegas Ranger District, 505-757-6121
Activities: Fishing
Finding the campground: From Pecos, travel east 4 miles on New Mexico Highway 223. Turn north onto Forest Road 86 and go 4 miles to the campground.

About the campground: This is one of only two or three campgrounds near Pecos where you might be able to escape the crowds of other campers. The five sites here are largely overlooked due to road conditions and the simple fact that the camp isn't off of New Mexico 63, as most of the camps are. Try your luck fishing in Cow Creek, especially during spring runoffs when the water level is up.

2 Field Tract

Location: 6 miles north of Pecos
Sites: 20 sites for tents and RVs
Facilities: Vault toilets, tables, grills, drinking water, shelters
Fee per night: $$
Elevation: 7,400 feet
Management: Santa Fe National Forest, Pecos/Las Vegas Ranger District, 505-757-6121

Activities: Hiking, fishing
Finding the campground: From Pecos, travel 6 miles north on New Mexico Highway 63 to the campground.

About the campground: Field Tract is the elite campground near Pecos. But with only 14 developed sites plus six three-sided Adirondack shelters, it can be very difficult to find a spot open, even midweek. The rushing water of the Pecos River means that anglers keep this place hopping throughout the summer. The good news is that early fall camping is quite comfortable, especially if you're lucky enough to snag one of the shelters. Stone fireplaces make these sites a cozy retreat from the rest of the world even in a cold rain shower.

3 Holy Ghost

Location: 15.5 miles north of Pecos
Sites: 24 sites for tents and RVs
Facilities: Vault toilets, tables, grills, drinking water
Fee per night: $$
Elevation: 8,200 feet
Management: Santa Fe National Forest, Pecos/Las Vegas Ranger District, 505-757-6121
Activities: Hiking, fishing
Finding the campground: From Pecos, travel 12 miles north on New Mexico Highway 63 to Terrero. Turn northwest onto Forest Road 122 and go 3.5 miles to the campground.

About the campground: Holy Ghost has been recently updated with paved campsites and new restroom facilities. As a result, everyone wants to stay here, so come early. You won't be disappointed with the scenery. The camp sits in a wildflower meadow and offers fishing access to Holy Ghost Creek.

4 Iron Gate

Location: 19 miles north of Pecos
Sites: 14 sites for tents and RVs
Facilities: Vault toilets, tables, grills, corral
Fee per night: None
Elevation: 9,400 feet
Management: Santa Fe National Forest, Pecos/Las Vegas Ranger District, 505-757-6121
Activities: Hiking, horseback riding
Finding the campground: From Pecos, travel 19 miles north on New Mexico Highway 63 to the campground.

About the campground: You're gonna love this camp—if you can get there. Rough roads and sheer distance keep many away, but that means more peace and quiet for you. Bring the horses because there are corrals and plenty of trails into the Pecos Wilderness. Be sure to call ahead for road conditions.

5 Jack's Creek

Location: 18.5 miles north of Pecos
Sites: 39 sites for tents and RVs
Facilities: Vault toilets, tables, grills, drinking water, corral
Fee per night: $$
Elevation: 8,900
Management: Santa Fe National Forest, Pecos/Las Vegas Ranger District, 505-757-6121
Activities: Hiking, fishing, horseback riding
Finding the campground: From Pecos, travel 14 miles north on New Mexico Highway 63. Turn northeast onto Forest Road 223 and go 4.5 miles to the campground.

About the campground: There's hope that sites at this very popular campground will soon be on the reservation system. Currently only the two group areas can be reserved, but keep your fingers crossed for the rest. If you're planning a trip to the Pecos area, call the National Recreation Reservation Service at 877-444-6777 to check for the availability of reservable campsites.

If you do manage to get a site at Jack's Creek, you won't be disappointed. The campground was fully refurbished several years ago during a cleanup of potentially hazardous materials from the abandoned Terrero Mine. The benefit to campers is a large, comfortable campground. Besides fishing access to Jack's Creek, there are horse corrals and plenty of trails to explore.

6 Mora River

Location: 14.5 miles north of Pecos
Sites: Dispersed
Facilities: Vault toilets, tables, grills
Fee per night: None
Elevation: 8,000 feet
Management: Santa Fe National Forest, Pecos/Las Vegas Ranger District, 505-757-6121
Activities: Hiking, fishing
Finding the campground: From Pecos, travel 14.5 miles north on New Mexico Highway 63 to the campground.

About the campground: This primitive roadside camp is one of several along the Pecos River near Cowles. The spot is popular due to easy fishing access and the stunning forest scenery.

7 Willow Creek

Location: 13.5 miles north of Pecos
Sites: 20 sites for tents and RVs
Facilities: Vault toilets, tables, grills
Fee per night: None
Elevation: 8,000 feet
Management: Santa Fe National Forest, Pecos/Las Vegas Ranger District, 505-757-6121
Activities: Hiking, fishing
Finding the campground: From Pecos, travel 13.5 miles north on New Mexico Highway 63 to the campground.

About the campground: Though it lacks the newly paved roads of the larger campgrounds in the area, Willow Creek is still popular. Set in a dense pine forest, the sites are well spaced. Easy access from NM 63 makes this a very popular camp, so plan to arrive early to secure a spot.

Wildflowers dot the hillsides and roadways in this region of the state in late spring.

SANTA ROSA

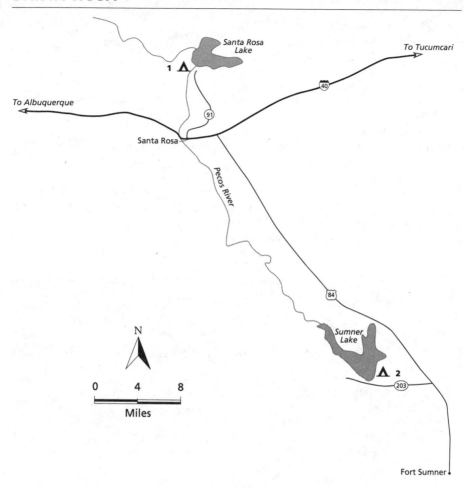

Santa Rosa specializes in two things: respite for the weary traveler and cool, clear waters for recreation and thrill seekers. As a stopover along historic U.S. Route 66, the town has its share of retro-design motels and roadside cafes. Sandwiched between these is a mix of modern chain motels and quaint Mexican food restaurants.

The word "oasis" is an understatement when referring to Santa Rosa—water is everywhere. Besides the Pecos River and its reservoirs, there are spring-fed ponds and natural playas. Of international renown to scuba divers is the Blue Hole, a spring-fed limestone shaft that reportedly is connected to Carlsbad Caverns, more than 200 miles away. The bottom of the shaft is now sealed with a locked grate buried beneath layers of silt, creating an 82-foot deep tank for diving. The water is cold but crystal clear, creating near-perfect conditions for dive training. A stop by Blue Hole is a nice diversion even for nondivers.

For more information:
Santa Rosa Chamber of Commerce
486 Parker Avenue
Santa Rosa, NM 88435
800-450-7084
http://www.santarosanm.com/

SANTA ROSA

	Group sites	RV sites	Total # of sites	Max. RV length	Hookups	Toilets	Showers	Drinking water	Dump station	Pets	Wheelchair	Recreation	Fee	Season	Can reserve	Stay limit
1 Santa Rosa Lake State Park	•	•	75		WE	F	•	•	•	•	•	HFB	$-$$			14
2 Sumner Lake State Park		•	•	90		WE	F	•	•	•	•	•	HFB	$-$$			14

Hookups: W = Water E = Electric S = Sewer
Toilets: F = Flush V = Vault P = Pit C = Chemical
Recreation: H = Hiking S = Swimming F = Fishing B = Boating L = Boat launch O = Off-highway driving R = Horseback riding
Maximum Trailer/RV Length given in feet. **Stay Limit** given in days. **Fee** $ = $0–5; $$ = $6–10; $$$ = $11–20.
If no entry under **Season,** campground is open all year. If no entry under **Fee,** camping is free.

1 Santa Rosa Lake State Park

Location: 7 miles north of Santa Rosa
Sites: 75 sites for tents and RVs
Facilities: Flush toilets, tables, grills, drinking water, visitor center, group sites, electricity, dump station, showers, hiking trails
Fee per night: $ to $$, annual permit available
Elevation: 4,800 feet
Management: New Mexico State Parks Department, 505-472-3110, www.emnrd.state.nm.us/nmparks
Activities: Hiking, fishing, boating, waterskiing, sailing, windsurfing
Finding the campground: From Santa Rosa, travel north 8 miles on New Mexico Highway 91 to the park.

About the campground: The campgrounds at this state park are set high on a bluff overlooking Santa Rosa Lake and offer outstanding views. You can enjoy all of the same activities here that are available at any of New Mexico's premier water sports lakes, but with surprisingly fewer people. The campgrounds are well-designed with plenty of space per site and all the usual amenities, including some sites with electricity.

2 Sumner Lake State Park

Location: 16 miles northwest of Fort Sumner
Sites: 90 sites for tents and RVs
Facilities: Flush and vault toilets, tables, grills, shelters, visitor center, group sites, showers, electricity, boat ramps and dock, dump station, drinking water
Fee per night: $ to $$, annual permit available
Elevation: 4,300 feet
Management: New Mexico State Parks Department, 505-355-2541, www.emnrd.state.nm.us/nmparks
Activities: Hiking, swimming, fishing, boating, waterskiing, sailing, windsurfing
Finding the campground: From Fort Sumner, travel north on U.S. Highway 84 about 16 miles. Turn west onto New Mexico Highway 203 and go 6 miles to the campground.

The campground: Tucked away in the Pecos River Valley south of Santa Rosa, this quiet lake is not heavily used, *yet*. With the numbers of water sports enthusiasts exploding yearly, they are bound to find Fort Sumner sooner or later.

There are four named campgrounds at Sumner Lake: East River, West River, East Side, and Main. East Side and Main offer lake access. Both of these include some sites with electricity, but only Main has comfort stations with flush toilets and showers. Sites are set amid juniper and mesquite, but shelters provide shade. Besides offering easy access to the lakeshore, these two campgrounds have views of the lake.

The river campgrounds–East River and West River–are on the backside of the dam, making them a quieter choice. River use is restricted to fishing only; no wading or floating is allowed. These sites are primitive but pleasant. In addition to the metal shelters, there are some shade trees along the river.

Southwest

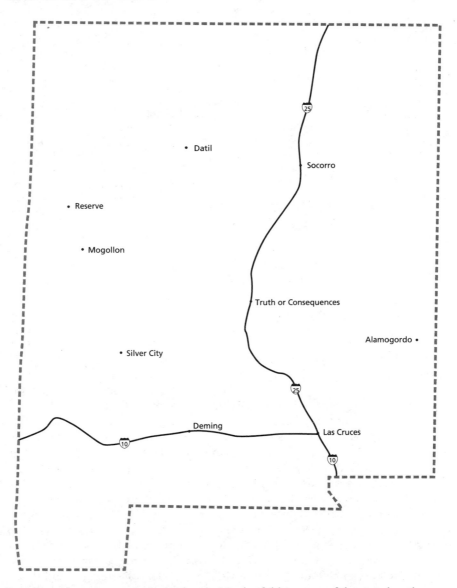

Loneliness here permeates even the air. Much of this corner of the state has the hushed feel of a ghost town. People are thinly scattered across the deserts and mountains, and though they welcome visitors, many choose to live here because the solitude suits them.

Activities in the region range from rock collecting at long forgotten mines to rock climbing in the Gila National Forest. You can fish the largest reservoirs in the state or crawl through ancient cliff dwellings. Just beware—the quiet of this place is addicting.

Socorro–Datil

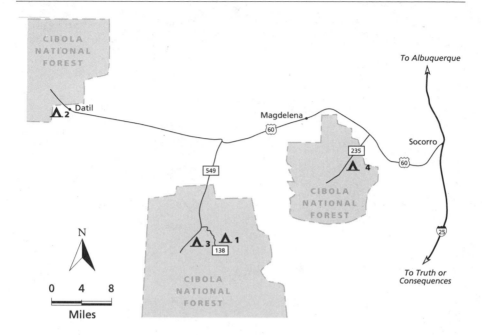

If your fondest desire is to be alone, this stretch of desert dotted with green mountains is a good place to end up. It wasn't always that way. Half a century ago, the area was a booming mining community. Today Socorro is home to the New Mexico Tech School of Mines. Farther west you'll find one of the most lonely but interesting places in the country: the National Radio Astronomy Observatory, Very Large Array Telescope (VLA). Using an array of 27 radio antennas, (picture giant satellite dishes), scientists here map the universe by capturing sound waves emitted by objects in space. Parts of the Jodie Foster movie "Contact" were filmed here, though the concept of "listening" to space in the movie was dramatized somewhat. Both the VLA and the School of Mines offer tours.

The Magdalena area was once a bustling mining community where fortunes were made and lost in the search for lead, copper, and even silver. Of interest to rock and mineral collectors are the abandoned mines, which allow collecting at their dump sites. Prize samples of vivid blue azurite, turquoise smithsonite, and green malachite can be found if you're willing to pay a collecting fee and spend a few hours sifting through the mine dumps. *The Rockhound's Guide to New Mexico*, by Falcon Publishing, has complete details.

For more information:

National Radio Astronomy Observatory VLA

P.O. Box 0

Socorro, NM 87801

505-835-7027

http://zia.aoc.nrao.edu/doc/vla/html/VLAhome.shtml

Magdalena Chamber of Commerce:
P.O. Box 281
Magdalena, NM 87825
505-854-2261

Socorro County Chamber of Commerce
P.O. Box 743
Socorro, NM 87801
505-835-0424

SOCORRO–DATIL

	Group sites	RV sites	Total # of sites	Max. RV length	Hookups	Toilets	Showers	Drinking water	Dump station	Pets	Wheelchair	Recreation	Fee	Season	Can reserve	Stay limit
1 Bear Trap			4	20		V				•		HO	Ø	May–Oct		14
2 Datil Well		•	22			V		•		•		H	$			14
3 Hughes Mill			2	20		V				•		HO	Ø	May–Oct		14
4 Water Canyon		•	4	22		V				•		HO ·	Ø	May–Oct		14

Hookups: W = Water E = Electric S = Sewer
Toilets: F = Flush V = Vault P = Pit C = Chemical
Recreation: H = Hiking S = Swimming F = Fishing B = Boating L = Boat launch O = Off-highway driving R = Horseback riding
Maximum Trailer/RV Length given in feet. **Stay Limit** given in days. **Fee** $ = $0–5; $$ = $6–10; $$$ = $11–20.
If no entry under **Season**, campground is open all year. If no entry under **Fee**, camping is free.

1 Bear Trap

Location: 30 miles southwest of Magdalena
Sites: 4 sites for tents
Facilities: Vault toilets, tables, grills
Fee per night: None
Elevation: 8,500 feet
Management: Cibola National Forest, Magdalena Ranger District, 505-854-2381
Activities: Hiking, four-wheel driving
Finding the campground: From Magdalena, travel west 15 miles on U.S. Highway 60. Turn south onto Forest Road 549 and go 12 miles. Turn east onto FR 138 and go 3 miles to the campground.

About the campground: By the time you get to this isolated campground, you may be wondering why they didn't call it "Camper Trap" instead. It is a very long and bumpy road to the campground, but at the end of the journey you'll find four quiet, streamside primitive sites that you can call home. You may encounter a few fellow travelers, but it's not likely.

The radio telescopes at the VLA site stretch skyward from the desert floor.

2 Datil Well

Location: Datil
Sites: 22 sites for tents and RVs
Facilities: Vault toilets, tables, grills, drinking water
Fee per night: $
Elevation: 7,400 feet
Management: Bureau of Land Management, Socorro Field Office, 505-835-0412
Activities: Hiking
Finding the campground: In Datil, travel west on U.S. Highway 60 to the campground (just past mile marker 77).

About the campground: This is a lovely spot to spend a night or two during your journey through southwest New Mexico. The sites are well spaced among low-growing piñon and juniper trees, with some very large pull-thru sites for big RV rigs.

3 Hughes Mill

Location: 30 miles southwest of Magdalena
Sites: 2 sites for tents
Facilities: Vault toilets, tables, grills
Fee per night: None
Elevation: 8,100 feet
Management: Cibola National Forest, Magdalena Ranger District, 505-854-2381
Activities: Hiking, four-wheel driving
Finding the campground: From Magdalena, travel west 15 miles on U.S. Highway 60. Turn south onto Forest Road 549 and go 15 miles to the campground.

About the campground: As with neighboring Bear Trap, the object of this game is just getting to the campground. If you can handle the long, rough road, then you deserve the quiet camp at the end of the journey. The trailhead for Mt. Withington Lookout is here, which makes it a bit more likely that you will encounter fellow humans, but you could just as easily have the place to yourself.

4 Water Canyon

Location: 19 miles southwest of Socorro
Sites: 4 sites for tents and RVs
Facilities: Vault toilets, tables, grills
Fee per night: None
Elevation: 6,800 feet
Management: Cibola National Forest, Magdalena Ranger District, 505-854-2381
Activities: Hiking, four-wheel driving, rock collecting, mountain biking

Finding the campground: From Socorro, travel west 13 miles on U.S. Highway 60. Turn south onto Forest Road 235 and go 6 miles to the campground.

About the campground: Don't come to this part of the state looking for deluxe remodeled campgrounds. Just come looking for quiet places to enjoy the outdoors. From Water Canyon you can drive, hike, bike, or climb to your heart's content with the Magdalena Mountains at your doorstep via trails and long-forgotten mining roads.

Collecting rocks and minerals at the abandoned mines is one form of recreation for campers at Water Canyon.

RESERVE–MOGOLLON

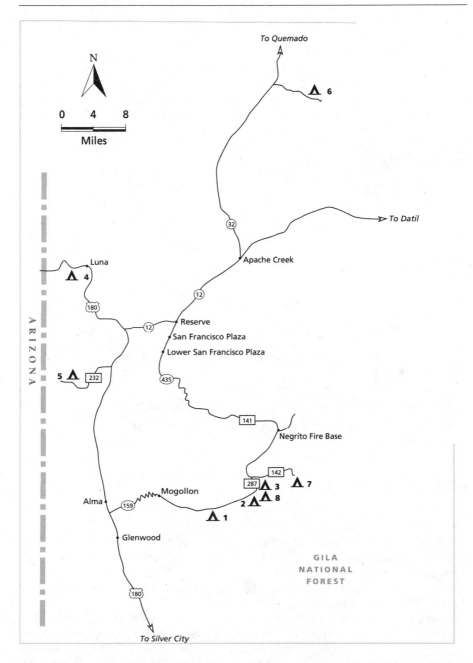

These two communities are located in Catron County, which boasts the lowest population per square mile of any county in the state. Believe it or not, even the campgrounds aren't crowded. Don't come here looking for the touristy side of New Mexico; there's probably not a Mexican-food restaurant in the whole county.

What you will find is beautiful country and miles of poorly maintained roads to explore. Bring a fishing pole and a good book and plan to stay awhile. It also wouldn't hurt to bring a winch in case you get stuck, because it will be a long wait for help in this county.

Reserve is the best place in the county to buy forgotten supplies or fuel. Mogollon, on the other hand, is more of a living museum than anything else. Located at the end of perhaps the state's narrowest, most winding paved road, it presents a colorful portrait of a mining past that still lives. Heed all warning signs concerning road conditions, or you'll need that winch.

RESERVE–MOGOLLON

		Group sites	RV sites	Total # of sites	Max. RV length	Hookups	Toilets	Showers	Drinking water	Dump station	Pets	Wheelchair	Recreation	Fee	Season	Can reserve	Stay limit
1	Ben Lilly		•	6	17		V				•		HF	Ø	May–Nov		14
2	Bursam			2			V				•		H	Ø	May–Oct		14
3	Gilita		•	6	17		V				•		HF	Ø	May–Nov		14
4	Head of the Ditch		•	2	30		V				•		HFR	Ø	Apr–Nov		14
5	Pueblo Park			7			V				•		H	Ø	May–Nov		14
6	Quemado Lake RA		•	62	30	E	V	•		•	•	•	FB	$$	Apr–Nov		14
7	Snow Lake (Dipping Vat)		•	40			V	•		•	•	•	HF	$	Apr–Nov		14
8	Willow Creek			6			V				•		HF	$$	Apr–Nov		14

Hookups: W = Water E = Electric S = Sewer
Toilets: F = Flush V = Vault P = Pit C = Chemical
Recreation: H = Hiking S = Swimming F = Fishing B = Boating L = Boat launch O = Off-highway driving R = Horseback riding
Maximum Trailer/RV Length given in feet. **Stay Limit** given in days. **Fee** $ = $0–5; $$ = $6–10; $$$ = $11–20.
If no entry under **Season,** campground is open all year. If no entry under **Fee,** camping is free.

1 Ben Lilly

Location: 30 miles east of Alma
Sites: 6 sites for tents and RVs
Facilities: Vault toilets, tables, grills
Fee per night: None
Elevation: 7,100 feet
Management: Gila National Forest, Reserve Ranger District, 505-533-6232
Activities: Hiking, fishing
Finding the campground: From U.S. Highway 180 south of Alma, turn east onto New Mexico Highway 159. Travel east 17 miles to Mogollon, then another 13 miles to the campground. From Reserve, the campground can be accessed via NM 435.

About the campground: As with all of the sites strung along Willow Creek, the attraction here is solitude. The only sounds are likely to be the stream and the wind in the pines. Getting here is quite a challenge but worth the trip if you like rough camping without having to hike to your camp.

2 Bursam

Location: 24 miles east of Alma
Sites: 2 sites for tents
Facilities: Vault toilets, tables, grills
Fee per night: None
Elevation: 7,100 feet
Management: Gila National Forest, Reserve Ranger District, 505-533-6232
Activities: Hiking
Finding the campground: From U.S. Highway 180 south of Alma, turn east onto New Mexico Highway 159. Travel east 17 miles to Mogollon, then another 7 miles to the campground.

About the campground: Bursam is the easiest campground on the loop from Reserve to Mogollon if you're coming from Mogollon. In fact, at times it is the only campground accessible from that direction. Other times it is inaccessible from either direction. Call ahead for road conditions or have a backup plan.

3 Gilita

Location: 32 miles east of Alma
Sites: 6 sites for tents and RVs
Facilities: Vault toilets, tables, grills
Fee per night: None
Elevation: 7,100 feet
Management: Gila National Forest, Reserve Ranger District, 505-533-6232
Activities: Hiking, fishing
Finding the campground: From U.S. Highway 180 south of Alma, turn east onto New Mexico Highway 159. Travel east 17 miles to Mogollon, then another 15 miles to the campground.

About the campground: If it's hard for you to believe that a campground in the woods at such a mild elevation wouldn't be a busy spot, you haven't been to this part of the state. The crowds are not here. Just peaceful pines and six streamside sites.

4 Head of the Ditch

Location: 2 miles west of Luna
Sites: 2 sites for tents and RVs
Facilities: Vault toilets
Fee per night: None
Management: Gila National Forest, Luna Work Station, 505-547-2612
Activities: Hiking, fishing, horseback riding, rock collecting
Finding the campground: From Luna, travel 2 miles west on U.S. Highway 180 to the campground entrance.

About the campground: You aren't in Arizona yet, but you can see it from the top of the hill. This tiny camp offers what few places in the state can offer: beautiful agates and even quartz geodes for those willing to search for them. The campground is usually empty of overnight visitors, but rockhounds from across the country often pass through here in search of mineral treasure. Fishing in the San Francisco River isn't a bad way to pass the time either.

5 Pueblo Park

Location: 18 miles southwest of Reserve
Sites: 7 sites for tents
Facilities: Vault toilets, tables, grills
Fee per night: None
Elevation: 7,000 feet
Management: Gila National Forest, Reserve Ranger District, 505-533-6232
Activities: Hiking, rock collecting
Finding the campground: From Reserve, travel 7.5 miles west on New Mexico Highway 12 to the junction with U.S. Highway 180. Turn south and go 6 miles. Turn west onto Forest Road 232 and go 6.5 miles to the campground.

About the campground: If you haven't figured it out yet, this area of the state is rich with mineral treasures which draw numerous rock collectors. This camp is no exception. Other than the rockhounds and the occasional hiker, Pueblo Park sees little use. It is a beautiful spot from which to enjoy the rugged scenery.

6 Quemado Lake Recreation Area

Location: 23 miles south of Quemado
Sites: 62 for tents and RVs
Facilities: Vault toilets, tables, grills, electricity, drinking water
Fee per night: $$
Elevation: 7,800 feet
Management: Gila National Forest, Quemado Ranger District, 505-773-4678
Activities: Fishing, boating
Finding the campground: From Quemado, travel 1 mile west on U.S. Highway 60. Turn south onto New Mexico Highway 32 and go 13 miles to Forest Road 13. Turn east and follow the signs to the campgrounds.

About the campground: This is the most developed recreational area in the entire region. Two campgrounds overlook the 130-acre lake. Juniper is the larger, with 40 sites, including 18 electric hookup sites. The electricity comes at the price of closeness to your neighbors, but the extra convenience is nice. Piñon campground has 22 additional sites suitable for tents or small trailers. Both campgrounds are modern and well maintained.

Fishing this lake is best accomplished by boat, but only electric motors are allowed. Even though it is the only place you're likely to find a crowd in all of Catron County, it's a pretty spot and easily accessed.

7 Snow Lake (Dipping Vat)

Location: 50 miles southeast of Reserve
Sites: 40 sites for tents and RVs
Facilities: Vault toilets, tables, grills
Fee per night: $
Elevation: 7,300 feet
Management: Gila National Forest, Reserve Ranger District, 505-533-6232
Activities: Hiking, fishing,
Finding the campground: From Reserve, travel 44 miles south on New Mexico Highway 435 (which becomes Forest Road 141). Turn east onto FR 142 and go another 6 miles to the campground.

About the campground: There are two kinds of campers in this world, and you can usually tell the difference by the amount of road dust on the outside (and the inside) of their vehicles. If you're the dusty type who will travel any road if there's a promise of a great camping spot, then Snow Lake is for you. The campground is in a light pine forest perched on a hill overlooking the pretty lake. Overall, it's a nice place to camp if you can handle the road.

Idyllic campsites with views of the water are the standard at Snow Lake.

8 Willow Creek

Location: 31 miles east of Alma
Sites: 6 sites for tents
Facilities: Vault toilets, tables, grills
Fee per night: $$
Elevation: 8,000 feet
Management: Gila National Forest, Reserve Ranger District, 505-533-6232
Activities: Fishing, hiking
Finding the campground: From U.S. Highway 180 south of Alma turn east onto New Mexico Highway 159. Travel east 17 miles to Mogollon, then another 16 miles to the campground.

About the campground: "Quiet" and "secluded" are the best words to describe this appropriately named camp. All of the six sites have access to Willow Creek and trails into the Gila Wilderness are a short distance away.

TRUTH OR CONSEQUENCES

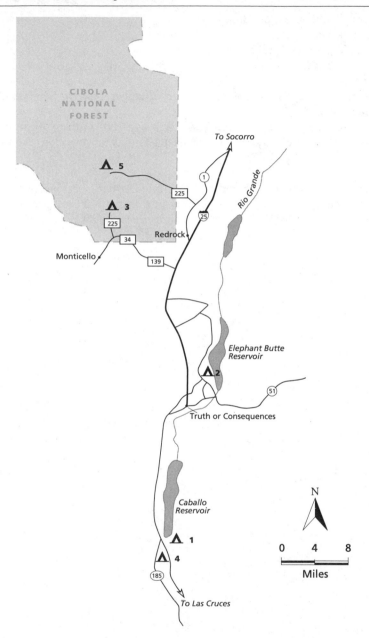

Truth or Consequences bills itself as a Southwestern recreation paradise. While that may be a bit of an exaggeration, the area does have the big advantage of being sandwiched between two of the state's most popular water sports lakes. The scenery is pure Southwest: red bluffs and cactus, with a faint blue line of mountains on the distant horizon.

In their rush to get to the lakes many people often overlook the fun things to do in town. Before the name changed to the distinctive "T or C," the town was called "Hot Springs." The historic bathhouse and spa district, where you can soak away your cares in the healing mineral waters is located downtown. It makes a nice break from all the activity at the lake campgrounds.

Another diversion away from the state parks is rock collecting. As with many areas of the state, rockhounds come here looking for unusual finds. In the Caballo Mountains the treasure includes carnelian, a vivid orange agate that polishes into exquisite jewelry.

For more information:
P.O. Box 31
Truth or Consequences, NM 87901
505-894-3536
800-831-9487

Truth or Consequences

		Group sites	RV sites	Total # of sites	Max. RV length	Hookups	Toilets	Showers	Drinking water	Dump station	Pets	Wheelchair	Recreation	Fee	Season	Can reserve	Stay limit
1	Caballo Lake State Park	•	•	136		WE	F	•	•	•	•	•	HFBL	$-$$			14
2	Elephant Butte Lake S.P.	•	•	111		WE	F	•	•	•	•	•	HFBL	$-$$		•	14
3	Luna Park			3			V				•		HR	Ø	Apr–Nov		14
4	Percha Dam State Park		•	29		WE	F	•	•		•	•	HF	$-$$			14
5	Springtime			6			V				•		HO	$	May–Oct		14

Hookups: W = Water E = Electric S = Sewer
Toilets: F = Flush V = Vault P = Pit C = Chemical
Recreation: H = Hiking S = Swimming F = Fishing B = Boating L = Boat launch O = Off-highway driving R = Horseback riding
Maximum Trailer/RV Length given in feet. **Stay Limit** given in days. **Fee** $ = $0–5; $$ = $6–10; $$$ = $11–20.
If no entry under **Season**, campground is open all year. If no entry under **Fee**, camping is free.

1 Caballo Lake State Park

Location: 16 miles south of Truth or Consequences
Sites: 136 sites for tents and RVs
Facilities: Flush toilets, tables, grills, drinking water, visitor center, group sites, electricity, dump station, showers, marina, playground, hiking trails
Fee per night: $ to $$, annual permit available
Elevation: 4,100 feet
Management: New Mexico State Parks Department, 505-743-3942, www.emnrd.state.nm.us/nmparks
Activities: Hiking, fishing, boating, waterskiing, sailing, windsurfing
Finding the campground: From I-25 south of Truth or Consequences, take exit 59 and follow the signs east to the park.

About the campground: The 136 sites here are spread among five campgrounds, four near the lake and one on the river behind the dam. If being on the lake isn't a higher priority, the riverside camp is the prettiest . There are more trees at this camp, and the rush of the water adds to the atmosphere.

If the fish aren't biting, the primitive roads on the east side of the lake lead to hours of exploration in the hills.

2 Elephant Butte Lake State Park

Location: 5 miles north of Truth or Consequences
Sites: 111 sites for tents and RVs
Facilities: Flush toilets, tables, grills, drinking water, visitor center, group sites, electricity, dump station, showers, playground, marina, hiking trails
Fee per night: $ to $$, annual permit available
Elevation: 4,500 feet
Management: New Mexico State Parks Department, 505-744-5421, www.emnrd.state.nm.us/nmparks
Reservations: Available at Desert Cove campground only, fee, 505-744-5421
Activities: Hiking, fishing, boating, waterskiing, sailing, windsurfing
Finding the campground: From Truth or Consequences, travel 3 miles east on New Mexico Highway 51. Turn north and follow the signs to the park.

About the campground: This state park is reportedly the third most popular spot in the state on Memorial Day weekend. So, quite simply, don't go there or at least not on that weekend. Other summer weekends may not be much better, but spring and fall are delightful. The campgrounds are not usually full to capacity and the temperature isn't unbearable.

The park offers plenty of diversion away from the water, including playgrounds and nature trails.

3 Luna Park

Location: 8 miles northeast of Monticello
Sites: 3 sites for tents only
Facilities: Vault toilets
Fee per night: None
Elevation: 7,400 feet
Management: Cibola National Forest, Magdalena Ranger District, 505-854-2381
Activities: Hiking, horseback riding
Finding the campground: From Monticello, travel north 5 miles on Forest Road 135/County Road 34. Turn north onto FR 225 and go 3 miles to the campground.

About the campground: This is a campground for lovers of off-road camping. The road into the campground is four-wheel drive only. The three spaces are situated amid lava beds at the foot of the San Mateo Mountains. It's hard to get here, but you'll likely have the place to yourself. Just don't come here looking for shade and bubbling brooks.

4 Percha Dam State Park

Location: 21 miles south of Truth or Consequences
Sites: 29 sites for tents and RVs
Facilities: Flush toilets, tables, grills, drinking water, group sites, electricity, showers, playground
Fee per night: $ to $$, annual permit available
Elevation: 4,100 feet
Management: New Mexico State Parks Department, 505-743-3942, www.emnrd.state.nm.us/nmparks
Activities: Hiking, fishing
Finding the campground: From I-25 south of Truth or Consequences, take exit 59 and follow the signs west to the park.

About the campground: Set amid towering cottonwoods, this unique state park offers a wonderful chance to hike and camp along the Rio Grande. Not usually as crowded as the two lakes to the north, Percha may be just the place for a bit of quiet contemplation.

5 Springtime

Location: 39 miles northwest of Truth or Consequences
Sites: 6 sites for tents
Facilities: Vault toilets
Fee per night: $
Elevation: 7,400 feet
Management: Cibola National Forest, Magdalena Ranger District, 505-854-2381
Activities: Hiking, four-wheel driving
Finding the campground: From Interstate 25 north of Truth or Consequences, take exit 100. Turn north onto New Mexico Highway 1 and go 4 miles. Turn west onto Forest Road 225 and go 12 miles to the campground.

About the campground: Ranked as one of the "Top 50 Campgrounds in New Mexico," by GreatOutdoors.com, Springtime is the only access camp near the Apache Kidd Wilderness. Hiking trails are near the camp. All six sites have Adirondack shelters, making this a comfortable place to camp even without a trailer (which cannot make the trip). The shelters are created so that a tent is not necessary; just bring a couple of tarps to stretch across the open side, and you'll have a cozy retreat.

The road is limited to high-clearance vehicles only. It would be wise to call ahead for specific road conditions.

SILVER CITY–GILA WILDERNESS

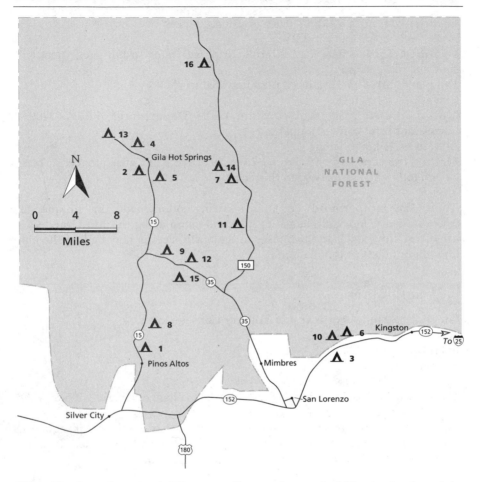

Silver City is aptly named. When you discover it, you feel like you've found the state's hidden treasure. There are dozens of things to do here, ranging from tours of the huge copper mines to hiking in the Gila. Try stopping for a drink at a real Western saloon at Piños Altos or visit the Billy the Kid jail site. The people here love to tell about the city's history and visitors are welcomed with open arms.

The Gila National Forest (locally shortened to "the Gila") is home to the first official wilderness area in the nation. The Gila Wilderness was created in 1924 to protect and preserve the incredible beauty found here. Once you've experienced the Gila, you'll agree it is an awe-inspiring national treasure.

For more information:
Grant County Chamber of Commerce
1103 N. Hudson Street
Silver City, NM 88061
505-538-3785
800-548-9378
www.silvercitynm.com

SILVER CITY–GILA WILDERNESS

		Group sites	RV sites	Total # of sites	Max. RV length	Hookups	Toilets	Showers	Drinking water	Dump station	Pets	Wheelchair	Recreation	Fee	Season	Can reserve	Stay limit
1	Cherry Creek			12			V				•		H	$$	May–Oct		14
2	Forks		•	D			V				•		HF	$	May–Oct		14
3	Gallinas			D			V				•		H	$	May–Oct		14
4	Gila Cliff Dwellings		•	12			F	•			•		H	$$	May–Oct		14
5	Grapevine		•	D			V				•		HF	$	May–Oct		14
6	Iron Creek		•	15	17		V				•		HF	$	May–Oct		14
7	Lower Black Canyon		•	3	17		V				•		H	$	May–Oct		14
8	McMillan			3			V				•		H	$	May–Oct		14
9	Mesa		•	24			V		•		•		HFB	$$	May–Oct		14
10	Railroad Canyon			D			V				•		H	Ø	May–Oct		14
11	Rocky Canyon		•	2	17		V				•		H	Ø	May–Oct		14
12	Sapillo/Lake Roberts	•	•	10			V				•		HFR	Ø			14
13	Scorpion TJ Corral		•	10	17		V	•			•		HF	Ø	May–Oct		14
14	Upper Black Canyon		•	2	22		V	•			•	•	HF	$	May–Oct		14
15	Upper End		•	10			V	•			•	•	HFB	$	May–Oct		14
16	Wall Lake			D			V				•		HF	$	May–Oct		14

Hookups: W = Water E = Electric S = Sewer
Toilets: F = Flush V = Vault P = Pit C = Chemical
Recreation: H = Hiking S = Swimming F = Fishing B = Boating L = Boat launch O = Off-highway driving R = Horseback riding
Maximum Trailer/RV Length given in feet. **Stay Limit** given in days. **Fee** $ = $0–5; $$ = $6–10; $$$ = $11–20.
If no entry under **Season**, campground is open all year. If no entry under **Fee**, camping is free.

1 Cherry Creek

Location: 9 miles northeast of Silver City
Sites: 12 sites for tents
Facilities: Vault toilets, tables, grills
Fee per night: $$
Elevation: 6,800 feet
Management: Gila National Forest, Silver City Ranger District, 505-388-8201
Activities: Hiking
Finding the campground: From Silver City, travel 9 miles north on New Mexico Highway 15 to the campground.

About the campground: Cherry Creek is a nice stopover on your way deeper into the Gila. The sites are in a light pine forest next to Cherry Creek, which is fishable during spring thaw.

2 Forks

Location: 1 mile south of Gila Hot Springs
Sites: Dispersed
Facilities: Vault toilets
Fee per night: $
Elevation: 5,700 feet
Management: Gila National Forest, Wilderness Ranger District, 505-536-2250
Activities: Hiking, fishing
Finding the campground: From Gila Hot Springs, travel south 1 mile on New Mexico Highway 15 to the campground.

About the campground: Forks is situated at the junction of the three forks of the Gila River. The campsites are scattered among cottonwoods and low shrubs, with easy access to the rushing waters of the river. From here, it's easy to see the attraction for the ancient people who called the Gila Valley their home.

3 Gallinas

Location: 10 miles west of Kingston
Sites: Dispersed
Facilities: Vault toilets
Fee per night: $
Elevation: 7,300 feet
Management: Gila National Forest, Wilderness Ranger District, 505-536-2250
Activities: Hiking
Finding the campground: From Kingston, travel 10 miles west on New Mexico Highway 152 to the campground.

About the campground: Rough camping in this stretch of the Mimbres Mountains brings the area's mining history to life. Abandoned slag piles and mineshafts turn up everywhere you look. Spend a little time on these piles and you never know what you may discover.

4 Gila Cliff Dwellings

Location: 3 miles north of Gila Hot Springs
Sites: 12 sites for tents and RVs
Facilities: Vault toilets, tables, grills , drinking water
Fee per night: $$
Elevation: 5,700 feet
Management: Gila National Forest, Wilderness Ranger District, 505-536-2250
Activities: Hiking
Finding the campground: From Gila Hot Springs, travel 3 miles north on New Mexico Highway 15 to the campground.

About the campground: The RV sites nearest the Gila Cliff Dwellings National Monument visitor center provide easy access to the monument and nearby trails but little else in the way of amenities. It's still a nice place to spend time, especially if you're bringing a group to tour the ruins.

A short hike from camp leads to these well-preserved cliff dwellings.

5 Grapevine

Location: 2 miles south of Gila Hot Springs
Sites: Dispersed
Facilities: Vault toilets
Fee per night: $
Elevation: 5,700 feet
Management: Gila National Forest, Wilderness Ranger District, 505-536-2250
Activities: Hiking, fishing, rock collecting
Finding the campground: From Gila Hot Springs, travel south 2 miles on New Mexico Highway 15 to the campground.

About the campground: Like the neighboring Forks campground, the sites here are scattered along the three forks of the Gila River. The valley is thick with cottonwood trees, providing plenty of shade from the summer sun. Camp here to fully appreciate the quiet of the Gila.

6 Iron Creek

Location: 10 miles west of Kingston
Sites: 15 sites for tents and RVs
Facilities: Vault toilets, tables, grills
Fee per night: $
Elevation: 7,300 feet
Management: Gila National Forest, Wilderness Ranger District, 505-536-2250
Activities: Hiking, fishing, rock collecting
Finding the campground: From Kingston, travel 10 miles west on New Mexico Highway 152 to the campground.

About the campground: The mere name of this campground evokes visions of miners laboring away trying to find that one streak of precious mineral hidden amid the slag. The creek is tiny but adds to the quiet atmosphere of this valley. Hiking trails lead from here into the Aldo Leopold Wilderness.

Campsites line the forks of the Gila River at the campgrounds near the cliff dwellings.

7 Lower Black Canyon

Location: 25 miles north of Mimbres
Sites: 3 sites for tents and RVs
Facilities: Vault toilets
Fee per night: $
Elevation: 7,200 feet
Management: Gila National Forest, Wilderness Ranger District, 505-536-2250
Activities: Hiking
Finding the campground: From Mimbres, travel 10 miles northwest on New Mexico Highway 35. Turn north onto Forest Road 150 and go 15 miles to the campground.

About the campground: These three primitive sites are the next best things to off-road camping you'll find in the Gila without lugging a backpack. Here you can escape the crowds below and enjoy the wildness of the place.

8 McMillan

Location: 11 miles northeast of Silver City
Sites: 3 sites for tents
Facilities: Vault toilets
Fee per night: $
Elevation: 6,800 feet
Management: Gila National Forest, Silver City Ranger District, 505-388-8201
Activities: Hiking
Finding the campground: From Silver City, travel 9 miles north on New Mexico Highway 15 to the campground.

About the campground: Like nearby Cherry Creek, McMillan makes a good place to begin or end your journey into the Gila. Consider this camp for a first night if you will be arriving after dark. The narrow, steep roads in the Gila aren't the best place to test either your brakes or your night vision.

9 Mesa

Location: 23 miles northeast of Silver City
Sites: 24 sites for tents and RVs
Facilities: Vault toilets, tables, grills, drinking water
Fee per night: $$
Elevation: 6,100 feet
Management: Gila National Forest, Wilderness Ranger District, 505-536-2250
Activities: Hiking, fishing, boating
Finding the campground: From Silver City, travel 23 miles north on New Mexico Highway 15 to the campground.

About the campground: Located on the shores of Lake Roberts, this camp is probably the most popular in the Gila National Forest. Pine trees tower over the campsites, and the 72-acre lake makes a beautiful backdrop. Plan to spend some time here.

10 Railroad Canyon

Location: 8 miles west of Kingston
Sites: Dispersed
Facilities: Vault toilets
Fee per night: None
Elevation: 7,300 feet
Management: Gila National Forest, Wilderness Ranger District, 505-536-2250
Activities: Hiking
Finding the campground: From Kingston, travel 10 miles west on New Mexico Highway 152 to the campground.

About the campground: Primitive sites here absorb the overflow from the Iron Creek camp. You may simply prefer the wider spacing of the primitive sites. The minerals in the mine dumps and the hiking in the Aldo Leopold Wilderness are the main attractions here.

11 Rocky Canyon

Location: 19 miles north of Mimbres
Sites: 2 sites for tents and RVs
Facilities: Vault toilets
Fee per night: None
Management: Gila National Forest, Wilderness Ranger District, 505-536-2250
Activities: Hiking
Finding the campground: From Mimbres, travel 10 miles northwest on New Mexico Highway 35. Turn north onto Forest Road 150 and go 9 miles to the campground.

About the campground: If you came to the Gila to get away from traffic noise and other people, try this tiny camp. The pines and oaks protect you from the summer sun and the peacefulness of the Gila shields you from the world.

12 Sapillo/Lake Roberts

Location: 24 miles northeast of Silver City
Sites: 10 sites for tents and RVs
Facilities: Vault toilets, tables, grills
Fee per night: None
Elevation: 6,100 feet
Management: Gila National Forest, Wilderness Ranger District, 505-536-2250
Activities: Hiking, fishing, horseback riding
Finding the campground: From Silver City, travel 24 miles north on New Mexico Highway 15 to the campground.

About the campground: This is another lakeside site at Lake Roberts. It makes an ideal base camp for enjoying all that the Gila has to offer. From here it's a short drive to the cliff dwellings or to trailheads into the wilderness. Riding stables are located nearby.

13 Scorpion TJ Corral

Location: 4 miles north of Gila Hot Springs
Sites: 10 sites for tents and RVs
Facilities: Vault toilets, tables, grills, drinking water
Fee per night: None
Elevation: 5,700 feet
Management: Gila National Forest, Wilderness Ranger District, 505-536-2250
Activities: Hiking, fishing
Finding the campground: From Gila Hot Springs, travel 4 miles north on New Mexico Highway 15 to the campground.

About the campground: These 10 sites provide easy access to the cliff dwellings, hiking trails, and the river. The setting is peaceful, with sites shaded by cottonwoods.

14 Upper Black Canyon

Location: 22 miles north of Mimbres
Sites: 2 sites for tents and RVs
Facilities: Vault toilets, tables, grills , drinking water
Fee per night: $
Management: Gila National Forest, Wilderness Ranger District, 505-536-2250
Activities: Hiking, fishing

Finding the campground: From Mimbres, travel 10 miles northwest on New Mexico Highway 35. Turn north onto Forest Road 150 and go 22 miles to the campground.

About the campground: Upper Black Canyon offers just one more opportunity to hide yourself away in the Gila. With only two sites here, the likelihood of crossing the path of another person is small. Just bring a comfortable lawn chair and enjoy.

15 Upper End

Location: 25 miles northeast of Silver City
Sites: 10 sites for tents
Facilities: Vault toilets, tables, grills, drinking water
Fee per night: $
Elevation: 6,100 feet
Management: Gila National Forest, Wilderness Ranger District, 505-536-2250
Activities: Hiking, fishing, boating
Finding the campground: From Silver City, travel 25 miles north on New Mexico Highway 15 to the campground.

About the campground: Upper End is set among the Ponderosa pines and oaks near Lake Roberts. The sites are nicely spaced for privacy, and this campground isn't as likely to fill on weekends as the two camps directly on the lake.

16 Wall Lake

Location: 37 miles north of Mimbres
Sites: Dispersed
Facilities: Vault toilets, tables
Fee per night: $
Elevation: 7,500 feet
Management: New Mexico Game & Fish Department, Southwest Office, 505-522-9796
Activities: Hiking, fishing
Finding the campground: From Mimbres, travel 10 miles northwest on New Mexico Highway 35. Turn north onto Forest Road 150 and go 27 miles to the campground.

About the campground: This is another of those dusty-road lakes. If you will travel almost any road to find the treasure waiting at the end, you will love Wall Lake. The tiny lake is well stocked with trout and is surrounded by the grandeur of the Gila. It's hard to imagine anything more satisfying.

DEMING–LAS CRUCES

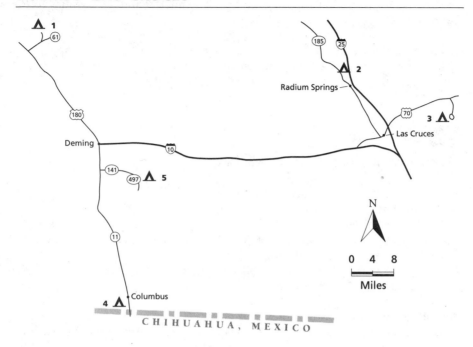

The area between and around Deming and Las Cruces is one of the most desolate parts of the state, but it has its own brand of rugged beauty. From agate collecting and rock climbing at the state parks to attending some of the state's best rock concerts at New Mexico State University, there's no shortage of things to do in the area. The diversity found here is best exhibited by the contrast between the tiny hamlet of Hatch, with its nationally renowned chili crop, and the White Sands Missile Range, with its array of scientific partners and guests.

Camping here is not for the faint of heart or for those seeking the gentle beauty of pine-covered mountains. Come here looking for a challenge, both physical and mental, and you won't leave disappointed.

For more information:
Deming Chamber of Commerce
P.O. Box 8
800 E. Pine
Deming, NM 88031
505-546-2674

Las Cruces Convention & Visitors Bureau
311 N. Downtown Mall
Las Cruces, NM 88001
505-524-8521
800-FIESTAS
www.lascruces.org/chamber

Hatch
P.O. Box 38
Hatch, NM 87937
505-267-5050

DEMING–LAS CRUCES

	Group sites	RV sites	Total # of sites	Max. RV length	Hookups	Toilets	Showers	Drinking water	Dump station	Pets	Wheelchair	Recreation	Fee	Season	Can reserve	Stay limit
1 City of Rocks State Park		•	57		WE	F	•	•		•	•	H	$-$$			14
2 Leasburg Dam State Park		•	29		WE	F	•	•	•	•	•	HF	$-$$			14
3 Organ Mountains			D			V		•		•	•	HR	Ø			14
4 Pancho Villa State Park	•	•	61		WE	F	•	•	•	•	•	H	$-$$			14
5 Rockhound State Park	•	•	36		WE	F	•	•	•	•	•	H	$-$$			14

Hookups: W = Water E = Electric S = Sewer
Toilets: F = Flush V = Vault P = Pit C = Chemical
Recreation: H = Hiking S = Swimming F = Fishing B = Boating L = Boat launch O = Off-highway driving R = Horseback riding
Maximum Trailer/RV Length given in feet. **Stay Limit** given in days. **Fee** $ = $0–5; $$ = $6–10; $$$ = $11–20.
If no entry under **Season,** campground is open all year. If no entry under **Fee,** camping is free.

---

1 City of Rocks State Park

Location: 28 miles northeast of Deming
Sites: 57 sites for tents and RVs
Facilities: Flush toilets, tables, grills, drinking water, visitor center, electricity, showers, hiking trails
Fee per night: $ to $$, annual permit available
Elevation: 5,200 feet
Management: New Mexico State Parks Department, 505-536-2800, www.emnrd.state.nm.us/nmparks
Activities: Hiking
Finding the campground: From Deming, travel 23 miles northwest on U.S. Highway 180. Turn east onto New Mexico Highway 61 and go 3 miles to the park access road.

About the campground: Begin your journey through New Mexico's almost forgotten region by enjoying the unusual rock formations at City of Rocks. The towers are carved from layers of volcanic ash weathered by wind and water. The campground puts you right in the heart of the park so you can enjoy the scenery. Just don't expect much in the way of creature comforts, like shade. Only 10 of the sites have electricity, so even the cool of an air conditioner will be hard to come by here.

2 Leasburg Dam State Park

Location: 15 miles north of Las Cruces
Sites: 29 sites for tents and RVs
Facilities: Flush toilets, tables, grills, drinking water, visitor center, group sites, electricity, dump station, showers, playground, hiking trails
Fee per night: $ to $$, annual permit available
Elevation: 4,200 feet
Management: New Mexico State Parks Department, 505-524-4068, www.emnrd.state.nm.us/nmparks
Activities: Hiking, fishing, waterskiing, sailing, windsurfing.
Finding the campground: From Las Cruces, travel 15 miles north on New Mexico Highway 185 to Radium Springs, then follow the signs to the park.

About the campground: The oasis created by the Leasburg diversion dam is a cool retreat from the desert. The park offers canoeing and kayaking in addition to fishing and floating. Bring an innertube.

3 Organ Mountains Recreation Area

Location: 20 miles east of Las Cruces
Sites: Dispersed
Facilities: Vault toilets, tables, grills, drinking water, visitor center, wheelchair-accessible facilities
Fee per night: None
Elevation: 5,700 feet
Management: Bureau of Land Management- Mimbres Office, 505-525-4300
Activities: Hiking, horseback riding
Finding the campground: From Las Cruces, travel east 17 miles on U.S. Highway 70. Turn south on Dripping Springs Road and follow the signs about 3 miles to the campground.

About the campground: If you've ever looked at jagged desert mountains and wondered what camping in such a harsh place would be like, here's your opportunity. Campgrounds in the Organ Mountains have all the usual Bureau of Land Management amenities, and you can enjoy the rugged beauty of these high, desert peaks.

4 Pancho Villa State Park

Location: 35 miles south of Deming
Sites: 61 sites for tents and RVs
Facilities: Flush toilets, tables, grills, drinking water, visitor center, group sites, electricity, showers, playground, hiking trails
Fee per night: $ to $$, annual permit available
Elevation: 4,000 feet

Management: New Mexico State Parks Department, 505-531-2711, www.emnrd.state.nm.us/nmparks
Activities: Hiking, scenic driving
Finding the campground: From Deming, travel 32 miles south on New Mexico Highway 11 to the park.

About the campground: There's no other place in New Mexico quite like Pancho Villa State Park. Picture cactus so dense that only the roads, trails, trailer parking pads, and the picnic tables remain free of their prickly dominance. More than thirty varieties thrive here. The best time to visit is late spring when the cacti explode with colorful blooms.

The other interesting feature here is the history. The park marks the last time mainland America was invaded by a foreign power. General Pancho Villa (a leader of the Mexican Revolution) attacked the U.S. Army post at Columbus in March 1916. In defense, the U.S. Army used air power and mechanized vehicles; the first time such tools were employed by the U.S. military.

5 Rockhound State Park

Location: 14 miles southeast of Deming
Sites: 36 sites for tents and RVs
Facilities: Flush toilets, tables, grills, drinking water, visitor center, group sites, electricity, dump station, showers, playground, hiking trails
Fee per night: $ to $$, annual permit available
Elevation: 4,500 feet
Management: New Mexico State Parks Department, 505-546-6182, www.emnrd.state.nm.us/nmparks
Activities: Hiking, rock collecting
Finding the campground: From Deming, travel 5 miles south on New Mexico Highway 11. Turn east onto NM 141 and go 6 miles. Turn southeast onto NM 497 and follow the signs to the park.

About the campground: Plenty has been said about the beautiful agate and flint specimens found at this state park. It is unique in that it is the only state park that actually encourages visitors to gather rocks. Unfortunately, unless you are an expert rock climber, you aren't likely to find much more than slivers that may have been washed out of the mountains by spring rains. The prize pieces are found around 700 feet up in the jagged hills. The good news is that there is a rock shop just outside the park entrance where you can purchase examples of what you could not find for yourself.

There's also not much here in the way of creature comforts, like shade. The campground has recently been updated, but there's no escaping the fact that this is harsh country.

Alamagordo–Carrizozo–Cloudcroft

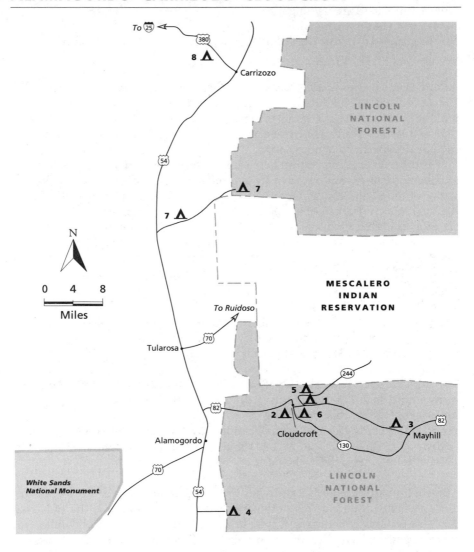

A 30-minute drive can take you from harsh desert to cool, pine-covered mountains. Of course, that's true in other places in the state, but the contrast is even greater here. At the foot of the Sacramento Mountains lies the White Sands National Monument. In spring you can romp in snow-white sand in one hour and in real snow the next. A little farther north another contrast exists in the Malpais lava beds, where you can camp atop bare lava rock one night and retreat into the aspens the next.

For more information:
Alamogordo Chamber of Commerce
P.O. Box 518
Alamogordo, NM 88310
505-437-6120
800-826-0294
800-545-4021
www.alamogordo.com

Carrizozo Chamber of Commerce
P.O. Box 567
Carrizozo, NM 88301
505-648-2472

Cloudcroft Chamber of Commerce
P.O. Box 1290
Cloudcroft, NM 88317
505-682-2733

ALMAGORDO–CARRIZOZO–CLOUDCROFT

		Group sites	RV sites	Total # of sites	Max. RV length	Hookups	Toilets	Showers	Drinking water	Dump station	Pets	Wheelchair	Recreation	Fee	Season	Can reserve	Stay limit
1	Apache			15			V	•		•			H	$	May–Sept		14
2	Deerhead		•	35			V	•		•			H	$$	May–Oct		14
3	James Canyon		•	5	16		V			•			H	Ø	Apr–Nov		14
4	Oliver Lee Memorial SP		•	44		WE	F	•	•	•	•	•	H	$-$$			14
5	Silver		•	32			V	•		•			H	$$	May–Nov		14
6	Sleepy Grass		•	45	16		V	•					HF	$$	May–Oct		14
7	Three Rivers		•	12			V	•		•			HR	$			14
8	Valley of Fires		•	12		E	V	•		•	•		H	$$			14

Hookups: W = Water   E = Electric   S = Sewer
Toilets: F = Flush   V = Vault   P = Pit   C = Chemical
Recreation: H = Hiking   S = Swimming   F = Fishing   B = Boating   L = Boat launch   O = Off-highway driving   R = Horseback riding
Maximum Trailer/RV Length given in feet. **Stay Limit** given in days. **Fee** $ = $0–5; $$ = $6–10; $$$ = $11–20.
If no entry under **Season**, campground is open all year. If no entry under **Fee**, camping is free.

Spring runoff in the mountains often produces spectacular results.

1 Apache

Location: 3 miles northeast of Cloudcroft
Sites: 15 sites for tents
Facilities: Vault toilets, tables, grills, drinking water
Fee per night: $
Elevation: 8,900 feet
Management: Lincoln National Forest, 505-682-2551
Activities: Hiking, scenic driving
Finding the campground: From Cloudcroft, travel 3 miles northeast on New Mexico Highway 244 to the campground.

About the campground: Apache is one of several roadside campgrounds near Cloudcroft that allows you to enjoy the lush forests of pine and aspen. The atmosphere is hushed, even when the crowds move in on weekends.

2 Deerhead

Location: 1 mile south of Cloudcroft
Sites: 35 sites for tents and RVs
Facilities: Vault toilets, tables, grills, drinking water
Fee per night: $$
Elevation: 8,700 feet
Management: Lincoln National Forest, 505-682-2551
Activities: Hiking, scenic driving
Finding the campground: From Cloudcroft, travel south 1 mile on New Mexico Highway 130 to the campground.

About the campground: Deerhead is located at the trailhead of the 21-mile Rim Trail, but the camp isn't overflowing with serious hikers. Perhaps a 21-mile hike is a bit too serious. The primary visitors here are West Texans looking for a place to escape the heat. The campground is lovely and designed to allow plenty of space for everyone.

3 James Canyon

Location: 2 miles northwest of Mayhill
Sites: 5 sites for tents and RVs
Facilities: Vault toilets, tables, grills
Fee per night: None
Elevation: 6,800 feet
Management: Lincoln National Forest, 505-682-2551
Activities: Hiking, scenic driving,
Finding the campground: From Mayhill, travel north on U.S Highway 82 to the campground.

About the campground: There are no streams to fish here, no trails to hike, just a pretty pine forest to soothe away your troubles. Snag one of these 5 sites for a relaxing getaway.

4 Oliver Lee Memorial State Park

Location: 10 miles south of Alamogordo
Sites: 44 sites for tents and RVs
Facilities: Flush toilets, tables, grills, drinking water, visitor center, electricity, dump station, showers, hiking trails
Fee per night: $ to $$, annual permit available
Elevation: 4,300 feet
Management: New Mexico State Parks Department, 505-437-8284, www.emnrd.state.nm.us/nmparks
Activities: Hiking
Finding the campground: From Alamogordo, travel 2 miles south on U.S. Highways 70/54. Turn southeast onto U.S. 54 and go 8.5 miles to the park entrance road.

About the campground: Oliver Lee is another of New Mexico's state parks that marks an historical landmark. In this case, it's the ranch of Oliver Milton Lee, one of the state's most colorful founders. The nice thing about these historical parks is that the state works hard at making them pleasant retreats for visitors. Oliver Lee is no exception. The surrounding area may be harsh, but parts of the park are lovely and green most of the year due to the waters of Dog Canyon Creek. Most of the campsites have sheltered picnic tables, providing much needed shade; many have electricity.

5 Silver

Location: 3 miles northeast of Cloudcroft
Sites: 32 sites for tents and RVs
Facilities: Vault toilets, tables, grills, drinking water, showers
Fee per night: $$
Elevation: 9,000 feet
Management: Lincoln National Forest, 505-682-2551
Activities: Hiking
Finding the campground: From Cloudcroft, travel 3 miles north on New Mexico Highway 244 to the campground.

About the campground: Anglers will find it difficult to believe that so many campgrounds near Cloudcroft stay so full, since none of them have fishing access. If the lack of trout doesn't bother you, come on up. The pines and aspen are waiting. Silver has an overflow area, which is nothing more than a gravel parking lot, but you'll appreciate it if you have to arrive late on the weekend—at least it's camping.

6 Sleepy Grass

Location: 1.5 miles south of Cloudcroft
Sites: 45 sites for tents and RVs
Facilities: Vault toilets, tables, grills, drinking water
Fee per night: $$
Elevation: 9,100 feet
Management: Lincoln National Forest, 505-682-2551
Activities: Hiking, fishing
Finding the campground: From Cloudcroft, travel 1 mile south on New Mexico Highway 130 to Forest Road 24B. Turn east and go about 1-half mile to the campground.

About the campground: The advantage this camp has over others in the Cloudcroft area is that it is just a bit off the road. That means two things—less traffic noise and fewer people. Unfortunately, the campground still fills on most summer weekends, so come early and ask the rangers to put this beautiful camp on the reservation system.

7 Three Rivers/Three Rivers Petroglyph National Recreation Site

Location: 30 miles south of Carrizozo
Sites: 12 sites for tents and RVs
Facilities: Vault toilets, tables, drinking water, corrals
Fee per night: $
Elevation: 5,000-6,800 feet
Management: Bureau of Land Management, Caballo Field Office, 505-525-4300 and Lincoln National Forest, Smokey Bear Ranger District, 505-257-4095
Activities: Hiking, horseback riding
Finding the campground: From Carrizozo, travel 25 miles south on U.S. Highway 54. Turn east onto Forest Road 579 and go 5 miles to the petroglyph site and another 8 miles to the Three Rivers campground.

About the campgrounds: There are camping facilities at the petroglyph site and at the edge of the White Mountain Wilderness. Both sites are situated in grasslands, with stunning views of the mountains to the east and the desert floor to the west. The national forest site is designed for horse campers, with trails leading into the wilderness area.

8 Valley of Fires Recreation Area

Location: 4 miles west of Carrizozo
Sites: 12 sites for tents and RVs
Facilities: Vault toilets, tables, grills, drinking water, electricity, wheelchair-accessible facilities
Fee per night: $$
Elevation: 5,100 feet
Management: National Park Service, 505-887-2241
Activities: Hiking
Finding the campground: From Carrizozo, travel 4 miles west on U.S. Highway 380 to the campground access road.

About the campground: Valley of Fires is for those looking for a camping experience that's a bit out of the ordinary. The campground sits atop the most recent lava flow in the continental United States. The experience is fascinating for natural science lovers. The lava beds are a wildlife habitat all their own. Even the squirrels that live on the flow are a different color than those living on the surrounding desert floor.

Southeast

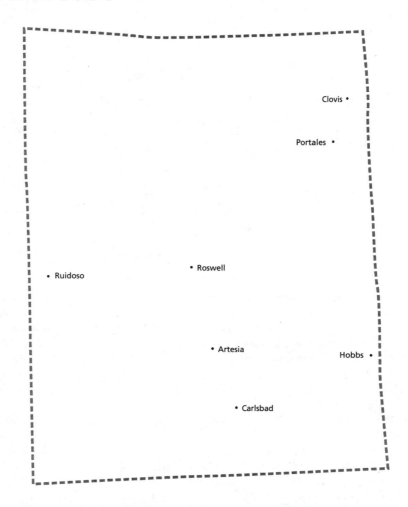

Throughout most of this quadrant of the state, the mountains are still a faint blue line teasing the horizon. But the rugged foothills hold a beauty all their own. There are jewels in the desert, like Carlsbad and Roswell.

The mountains break the rolling plains at the far western edge of the region. Summer and winter playgrounds at Ruidoso are the big attractions. Campgrounds are plentiful, as well as beautiful.

CLOVIS–PORTALES

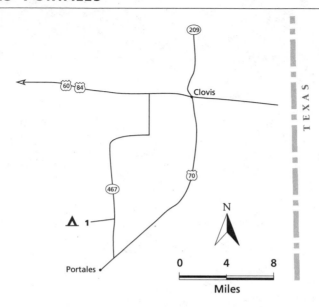

These two towns are gateways between Texas and New Mexico. They have a bit more in common with their Texas neighbors than with the rest of New Mexico. Agriculture (primarily cattle and dairy) provides the mainstay of both communities. Neither town is without some New Mexican charm, however. You just have to look past the Texas influences.

For more information:
Clovis/Curry County Chamber of Commerce
215 N. Main Street
Clovis, NM 88101
505-763-3435

Portales/Roosevelt County Chamber of Commerce
7th and Abilene
Portales, NM 88130
505-356-8541
800-635-8036

CLOVIS–PORTALES

	Group sites	RV sites	Total # of sites	Max. RV length	Hookups	Toilets	Showers	Drinking water	Dump station	Pets	Wheelchair	Recreation	Fee	Season	Can reserve	Stay limit
1 Oasis State Park		•	23		WE	F	•	•	•	•	•	HF	$-$$			14

Hookups: W = Water E = Electric S = Sewer
Toilets: F = Flush V = Vault P = Pit C = Chemical
Recreation: H = Hiking S = Swimming F = Fishing B = Boating L = Boat launch O = Off-highway driving R = Horseback riding
Maximum Trailer/RV Length given in feet. **Stay Limit** given in days. **Fee** $ = $0–5; $$ = $6–10; $$$ = $11–20.
If no entry under **Season,** campground is open all year. If no entry under **Fee,** camping is free.

---

1 Oasis State Park

Location: 6 miles north of Portales
Sites: 23 sites for tents and RVs, 13 with electricity
Facilities: Vault and flush toilets, tables, grills, some shelters, showers, some electrical hookups, playground, water, dump station, trails
Fee per night: $ to $$, annual permit available
Elevation: 4,010 feet
Management: New Mexico State Parks Department, 505-356-5331
Activities: Hiking, fishing, bird watching
Finding the campground: From Portales, travel north on New Mexico Highway 467 about 6 miles to the park access road. Turn west.

About the campground: This interesting little state park makes a wonderful stopover point as you travel into or out of New Mexico. There are plenty of cottonwoods to provide respite from the sun and a quiet pond for fishing. You won't find the park crowded except perhaps with locals picnicking on Sunday afternoons. Birders will find the spot ideal, as the pond is winter home to more than 80 different species.

Roswell–Ruidoso

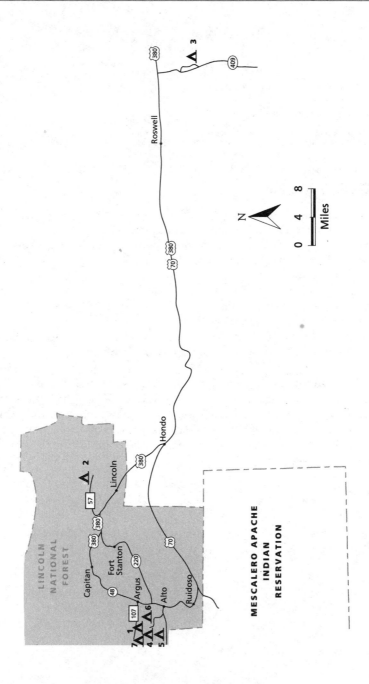

These two cities are connected by a long stretch of lonely road and not much else. Roswell is an oil town and the home of the New Mexico Military Institute. Two museums document Roswell's UFO claim to fame. Ruidoso is the playground in Roswell's backyard. With such attractions as a ski resort, horse racing, world-class golf courses, and access to the beautiful Sierra Blanca Mountains, Ruidoso attracts visitors from all over southeastern New Mexico and western Texas. Both cities boast enough activities to fill a long weekend.

For more information:

Roswell Convention and Visitors Bureau
P.O. Box 70
Roswell, NM 88202-0070
505-623-5695
www.roswellnm.org

Ruidoso Valley Chamber of Commerce
P.O. Box 698
Ruidoso, NM 88345
505-257-7395
800-253-2255

ROSWELL–RUIDOSO

	Group sites	RV sites	Total # of sites	Max. RV length	Hookups	Toilets	Showers	Drinking water	Dump station	Pets	Wheelchair	Recreation	Fee	Season	Can reserve	Stay limit
1 Argentina-Bonito		•	D			V					•	HR	$	May–Oct		14
2 Baca	••		D			V					•	H	Ø	May–Oct		14
3 Bottomless Lakes SP		•	11		WE	F	•	•	•	•	•	HFSB	$-$$			14
4 Monjeau			12			V					•	H	$	May–Oct		14
5 Oak Grove		•	29	18		V					•	H	$	May–Oct		14
6 Skyline		•	17			V					•	H	$	May–Oct		14
7 Southfork		•	60	20		V		•		•	•	HF	$$	May–Oct		14

Hookups: W = Water E = Electric S = Sewer
Toilets: F = Flush V = Vault P = Pit C = Chemical
Recreation: H = Hiking S = Swimming F = Fishing B = Boating L = Boat launch O = Off-highway driving R = Horseback riding
Maximum Trailer/RV Length given in feet. **Stay Limit** given in days. **Fee** $ = $0–5; $$ = $6–10; $$$ = $11–20.
If no entry under **Season**, campground is open all year. If no entry under **Fee**, camping is free.

1 Argentina–Bonito

Location: 18 miles northwest of Ruidoso
Sites: Dispersed
Facilities: Vault toilets
Fee per night: $
Elevation: 7,600 feet
Management: Lincoln National Forest, Smokey Bear Ranger District
505-257-4095

Activities: Hiking, horseback riding
Finding the campground: From Ruidoso, travel 10 miles north on New Mexico Highway 48. Turn west on Forest Road 107 and go 8 miles to the campground.

About the campground: Argentina-Bonito is not really a formal campground, but rather an area for primitive horseback camping; expect heavy use, especially during fall hunting seasons. The aspens and miles of trails and mining roads to explore are the main attractions for most equestrians.

2 Baca

Location: 17 miles east of Capitan
Sites: Dispersed
Facilities: Vault toilets
Fee per night: None
Elevation: 7,200 feet
Management: Lincoln National Forest, Smokey Bear Ranger District, 505-257-4095
Activities: Hiking
Finding the campground: From Capitan, travel 8 miles east on U.S. Highway 380. Turn north onto Forest Road 57 and go 9 miles to the campground.

About the campground: Tenters and people with small trailers might find that this is the perfect spot during summer months if they're just looking for a mountain getaway. There's not much to do here but kick back and relax. The advantage is that you might have the place all to yourself.

3 Bottomless Lakes State Park

Location: 16 miles southeast of Roswell
Sites: 11 sites for tents and RVs
Facilities: Flush toilets, tables, grills, drinking water, visitor center, group sites, electricity, dump station, showers, playground, hiking trails
Fee per night: $ to $$, annual permit available
Elevation: 3,500 feet
Management: New Mexico State Parks Department, 505-624-6058, www.emnrd.state.nm.us/nmparks
Activities: Hiking, swimming, fishing, boating
Finding the campground: From Roswell travel 10 miles east on U.S. Highway 380. Turn south onto New Mexico Highway 409 and go 6 miles to the park.

About the campground: Bottomless Lakes is another example of how the New Mexico state park system showcases the oddities of the state and combines them with recreational opportunities when it can. The lakes here are really sink-holes ranging in depth from 17 to 90 feet. Some are clear enough to attract scuba divers, but most are a murky, blue-green color. The camping facilities make this a nice stopover or a good point from which to enjoy the attractions in Roswell.

4 Monjeau

Location: 11 miles northwest of Ruidoso
Sites: 12 sites for tents
Facilities: Vault toilets, tables, grills
Fee per night: $
Elevation: 7,600 feet
Management: Lincoln National Forest, Smokey Bear Ranger District, 505-257-4095
Activities: Hiking
Finding the campground: From Ruidoso, travel 5 miles north on New Mexico Highway 48. Turn west onto Forest Road 127/NM 532 and go 1 mile. Turn north on FR 117 and go 5 miles to the campground.

About the campground: Monjeau is one of the prettiest campgrounds in the Lincoln National Forest. The camp was once a fire lookout. The only thing missing is a stream full of trout.

5 Oak Grove

Location: 9 miles northwest of Ruidoso
Sites: 29 sites for tents and RVs
Facilities: Vault toilets, tables, grills
Fee per night: $
Elevation: 8,400 feet
Management: Lincoln National Forest, Smokey Bear Ranger District, 505-257-4095
Activities: Hiking
Finding the campground: From Ruidoso, travel 5 miles north on New Mexico Highway 48. Turn west onto Forest Road 127/ NM 532 and go 4 miles to the campground.

About the campground: Oak Grove lives up to its name, as it sits in a mixed oak and aspen forest on the road to the Ski Apache resort. The 29 sites here will fill quickly in summer, and, unfortunately, this camp isn't on the reservation system. You'd be wise to arrive early or have an alternate plan.

6   Skyline

Location: 10 miles northwest of Ruidoso
Sites: 17 sites for tents and RVs
Facilities: Vault toilets, tables, grills
Fee per night: $
Elevation: 7,400 feet
Management: Lincoln National Forest, Smokey Bear Ranger District,
505-257-4095
Activities: Hiking
Finding the campground: From Ruidoso, travel 5 miles north on New Mexico
Highway 48. Turn west onto Forest Road 127/NM 532 and go 1 mile. Turn north
on FR 117 and go 4 miles to the campground.

About the campground: Skyline is a camp for lovers of windswept, wide-open
spaces. From this high perch you can hike above the timberline and enjoy the
vistas in all directions. "Breathtaking" doesn't even come close to describing the
views found here.

7   Southfork

Location: 14 miles northwest of Ruidoso
Sites: 60 sites for tents and RVs
Facilities: Vault toilets, tables, grills, drinking water
Fee per night: $$
Elevation: 7,500 feet
Management: Lincoln National Forest, Smokey Bear Ranger District,
505-257-4095
Activities: Hiking, fishing
Finding the campground: From Ruidoso, travel 10 miles north on New Mex-
ico Highway 48. Turn west on Forest Road 107 and go 4 miles to the camp-
ground.

About the campground: Southfork is no longer on the National Forest Reser-
vation System, but it should be. This is the most popular campground in the
Ruidoso area and even though it's the largest, spaces fill very early on summer
weekends. The big draw here is access to the shore of Bonito Lake. The crystal
clear waters are well stocked and fishing is usually excellent.

The campground itself is not well designed. Spaces are crowded together;
many are side-by-side, parking-lot style. Having said all that, it's still a nice place
to camp if you want to fish. Try a weekday visit to avoid the crowds.

LOVINGTON–HOBBS–ARTESIA–CARLSBAD

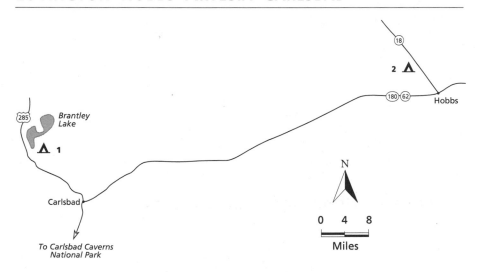

This is oil country. There are probably more pump jacks than people per square mile in this desolate region. With the exception of Carlsbad, these communities have little to attract visitors. Those who do come through are often surprised by what they find. The people are friendly and the food is good.

As for Carlsbad, the Carlsbad Caverns National Park is the big attraction. And rightly so. The park service works very hard to attract visitors by changing and upgrading its offerings. Recent changes include "wild" caving tours that allow you to experience parts of the main cavern and even other caves in the park despite the absence of paved trails and installed lights. There is no public vehicle camping in or around Carlsbad Caverns National Park, so check with commercial RV parks for camping accommodations.

For more information:
Lovington Chamber of Commerce
P.O. Box 1347
Lovington, NM 88260
505-396-5311

Artesia Chamber of Commerce
P.O. Box 99
Artesia, NM 88211
505-746-2744

Hobbs Chamber of Commerce
400 N. Marland
Hobbs, NM 88240
505-397-3202
800-658-6291

Carlsbad Convention and Visitors' Bureau
P.O. Box 910
Carlsbad, NM 88220
505-887-6516
800-221-1224
www.caverns.com/~chamber/sch-uni.htm

Carlsbad Caverns National Park
3225 National Parks Highway
Carlsbad, NM 88220
(505) 785-2232
http://www.nps.gov/cave/

LOVINGTON–HOBBS–ARTESIA–CARLSBAD

	Group sites	RV sites	Total # of sites	Max. RV length	Hookups	Toilets	Showers	Drinking water	Dump station	Pets	Wheelchair	Recreation	Fee	Season	Can reserve	Stay limit
1 Brantley Lake State Park	•	•	51		WE	F	•	•	•	•	•	HFB	$-$$			14
2 Harry McAdams State Park		•	23		WE	F	•	•	•	•			$-$$			

Hookups: W = Water E = Electric S = Sewer
Toilets: F = Flush V = Vault P = Pit C = Chemical
Recreation: H = Hiking S = Swimming F = Fishing B = Boating L = Boat launch O = Off-highway driving R = Horseback riding
Maximum Trailer/RV Length given in feet. **Stay Limit** given in days. **Fee** $ = $0–5; $$ = $6–10; $$$ = $11–20.
If no entry under **Season**, campground is open all year. If no entry under **Fee**, camping is free.

The nightly flight of the bats at Carlsbad is a sight to behold.

Giant formations like this one are abundant in the main cave at Carlsbad Caverns National Park.

▌ Brantley Lake State Park

Location: 12 miles north of Carlsbad
Sites: 51 sites for tents and RVs
Facilities: Flush toilets, tables, grills, drinking water, visitor center, group sites, electricity, dump station, showers, playground, hiking trails
Fee per night: $ to $$, annual permit available
Elevation: 3,300 feet
Management: New Mexico State Parks Department, 505-457-2384, www.emnrd.state.nm.us/nmparks
Activities: Hiking, fishing, boating, water skiing, sailing, windsurfing
Finding the campground: From Carlsbad, travel 10 miles north on U.S. Highway 285. Turn east onto the park access road and go 2 miles to the park.

About the campground: When you live in the desert Southwest, you take every opportunity you can to get wet. Brantley Lake is one of those watering holes that attracts locals by the dozens. It does make a nice stopover or a good base camp for exploring all that Carlsbad has to offer

▌ Harry McAdams State Park

Location: 4 miles northwest of Hobbs
Sites: 23 sites for tents and RVs
Facilities: Flush toilets, tables, grills, drinking water, electricity, dump station, showers
Fee per night: $ to $$, annual permit available
Elevation: 3,700 feet
Management: New Mexico State Parks Department, 505-392-5845
Activities: Golf, soaring (glider planes)
Finding the campground: From Hobbs, travel 6 miles north on New Mexico Highway 18. Turn west and follow the signs to the campground.

About the campground: Because Hobbs tends to be on the way to a number of other places, it is a popular stopover choice. Harry McAdams State Park is an ideal place to do just that. The sites are closely spaced in a grassy park. They are well maintained and many offer unimpeded views to the west, allowing campers to enjoy one of the treasures of southeastern New Mexico: glorious sunsets. There are a couple of bonuses here. One is the city-owned golf course next door. It's a cool oasis in the middle of the desert. The other is the Soaring Society of America Headquarters across the road. Even if you don't participate in this graceful air sport of glider planes, watching those who do makes for a pleasant way to pass the time before you head back on the road.

Index

About the Author

Camping New Mexico is Melinda Crow's fourth FalconGuide®. As an avid lifetime camper, and now as the owner of an RV resort in central Texas, Crow knows camping. Her own camping modes have ranged from tents to tent trailers, from pickup campers to plush RVs. Although she has camped across the entire southern United States, her favorite destinations are still found in New Mexico.

Other FalconGuides® written by Crow are Camping Colorado, Rockhounding Texas, and The Rockhound's Guide to New Mexico. Her magazine articles have appeared in Texas Highways, 3-2-1 Contact, Parenting, and Family Fun.

HIKING GUIDES

Best Hikes Along the Continental Divide
Hiking Alaska
Hiking Arizona
Hiking Arizona's Cactus Country
Hiking the Beartooths
Hiking Big Bend National Park
Hiking the Bob Marshall Country
Hiking California
Hiking California's Desert Parks
Hiking Carlsbad Caverns
    and Guadalupe Mtns. National Parks
Hiking Colorado
Hiking Colorado, Vol. II
Hiking Colorado's Summits
Hiking Colorado's Weminuche Wilderness
Hiking the Columbia River Gorge
Hiking Florida
Hiking Georgia
Hiking Glacier & Waterton Lakes National Parks
Hiking Grand Canyon National Park
Hiking Grand Staircase-Escalante/Glen Canyon
Hiking Grand Teton National Park
Hiking Great Basin National Park
Hiking Hot Springs in the Pacific Northwest
Hiking Idaho
Hiking Maine
Hiking Michigan
Hiking Minnesota
Hiking Montana
Hiking Mount Rainier National Park
Hiking Mount St. Helens
Hiking Nevada
Hiking New Hampshire

Hiking New Mexico
Hiking New York
Hiking the North Cascades
Hiking Northern Arizona
Hiking Olympic National Park
Hiking Oregon
Hiking Oregon's Eagle Cap Wilderness
Hiking Oregon's Mount Hood/Badger Creek
Hiking Oregon's Three Sisters Country
Hiking Pennsylvania
Hiking Ruins Seldom Seen
Hiking Shenandoah
Hiking the Sierra Nevada
Hiking South Carolina
Hiking South Dakota's Black Hills Country
Hiking Southern New England
Hiking Tennessee
Hiking Texas
Hiking Utah
Hiking Utah's Summits
Hiking Vermont
Hiking Virginia
Hiking Washington
Hiking Wisconsin
Hiking Wyoming
Hiking Wyoming's Cloud Peak Wilderness
Hiking Wyoming's Wind River Range
Hiking Yellowstone National Park
Hiking Zion & Bryce Canyon National Parks
Wild Montana
Wild Country Companion
Wild Utah
Wild Virginia

■ *To order any of these books, check with your local bookseller*
*or call FALCON ® at **1-800-582-2665**.*
Visit us on the world wide web at:
www.FalconOutdoors.com

FALCON®

FALCONGUIDES ® Leading the Way™

FALCONGUIDES ® are available for where-to-go hiking, mountain biking, rock climbing, walking, scenic driving, fishing, rockhounding, paddling, birding, wildlife viewing, and camping. We also have FalconGuides on essential outdoor skills and subjects and field identification. The following titles are currently available, but this list grows every year. For a free catalog with a complete list of titles, call FALCON toll-free at 1-800-582-2665.

MOUNTAIN BIKING GUIDES

Mountain Biking Arizona
Mountain Biking Colorado
Mountain Biking Georgia
Mountain Biking Idaho
Mountain Biking New Mexico
Mountain Biking New York
Mountain Biking Northern New England
Mountain Biking Oregon
Mountain Biking South Carolina
Mountain Biking Southern California
Mountain Biking Southern New England
Mountain Biking Utah
Mountain Biking Washington
Mountain Biking Wisconsin
Mountain Biking Wyoming

LOCAL CYCLING SERIES

Fat Trax Bozeman
Mountain Biking Albuquerque
Mountain Biking Bend
Mountain Biking Boise
Mountain Biking Chequamegon
Mountain Biking Chico
Mountain Biking Colorado Springs
Mountain Biking Denver/Boulder
Mountain Biking Durango
Mountain Biking Flagstaff and Sedona
Mountain Biking Helena
Mountain Biking Moab
Mountain Biking Spokane
Mountain Biking the Twin Cities
Mountain Biking Utah's St. George/Cedar City Area
Mountain Biking the White Mountains (West)

■ *To order any of these books, check with your local bookseller*
*or call FALCON ® at **1-800-582-2665**.*
Visit us on the world wide web at:
www.FalconOutdoors.com

FALCON®

WILDLIFE VIEWING GUIDES

Alaska Wildlife Viewing Guide
Arizona Wildlife Viewing Guide
California Wildlife Viewing Guide
Colorado Wildlife Viewing Guide
Florida Wildlife Viewing Guide
Indiana Wildlife Vewing Guide
Iowa Wildlife Viewing Guide
Kentucky Wildlife Viewing Guide
Massachusetts Wildlife Viewing Guide
Montana Wildlife Viewing Guide
Nebraska Wildlife Viewing Guide
Nevada Wildlife Viewing Guide
New Hampshire Wildlife Viewing Guide
New Jersey Wildlife Viewing Guide
New Mexico Wildlife Viewing Guide
New York Wildlife Viewing Guide
North Carolina Wildlife Viewing Guide
North Dakota Wildlife Viewing Guide
Ohio Wildlife Viewing Guide
Oregon Wildlife Viewing Guide
Puerto Rico and the Virgin Islands WVG
Tennessee Wildlife Viewing Guide
Texas Wildlife Viewing Guide
Utah Wildlife Viewing Guide
Vermont Wildlife Viewing Guide
Virginia Wildlife Viewing Guide
Washington Wildlife Viewing Guide
West Virginia Wildlife Viewing Guide
Wisconsin Wildlife Viewing Guide

HISTORIC TRAIL GUIDES

Traveling California's Gold Rush Country
Traveling the Lewis & Clark Trail
Traveling the Oregon Trail
Traveler's Guide to the Pony Express Trail

SCENIC DRIVING GUIDES

Scenic Driving Alaska and the Yukon
Scenic Driving Arizona
Scenic Driving the Beartooth Highway
Scenic Driving California
Scenic Driving Colorado
Scenic Driving Florida
Scenic Driving Georgia
Scenic Driving Hawaii
Scenic Driving Idaho
Scenic Driving Indiana
Scenic Driving Kentucky
Scenic Driving Michigan
Scenic Driving Minnesota
Scenic Driving Montana
Scenic Driving New England
Scenic Driving New Mexico
Scenic Driving North Carolina
Scenic Driving Oregon
Scenic Driving the Ozarks including the
   Ouchita Mountains
Scenic Driving Pennsylvania
Scenic Driving Texas
Scenic Driving Utah
Scenic Driving Virginia
Scenic Driving Washington
Scenic Driving Wisconsin
Scenic Driving Wyoming
Scenic Driving Yellowstone & Grand Teton
   National Parks
Back Country Byways
Scenic Byways East & South
Scenic Byways Far West
Scenic Byways Rocky Mountains

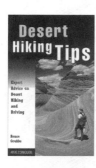

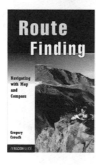